ROOKIE COACHES TENNIS GUIDE

American Coaching Effectiveness Program

in cooperation with the
United States Tennis Association

Leisure Press
Champaign, Illinois

Library of Congress Cataloging-in-Publication Data

American Coaching Effectiveness Program.
    Rookie coaches tennis guide / by American Coaching Effectiveness
Program in cooperation with the United States Tennis Association.
        p.   cm.
    ISBN 0-88011-420-7
    1. Tennis--Coaching.   I. United States Tennis Association.
II. Title.
GV1002.9.C63A45   1991
796.342'07'7--dc20   90-22335
                                                                        CIP

ISBN: 0-88011-420-7

Developmental Editor: Ted Miller
Tennis Consultant: Randy Hester, USTA Junior Tennis Coordinator
Assistant Editors: Dawn Levy, Julia Anderson, Valerie Hall
Copyeditor: Molly Bentsen
Proofreader: Terry Olive
Production Director: Ernie Noa
Typesetter: Brad Colson
Text Design: Keith Blomberg
Text Layout: Tara Welsch
Cover Design: Jack Davis
Cover Photo: Michael Pakash for the USTA
Illustrations: Keith Blomberg, Tim Stiles
Printer: United Graphics

Printed in the United States of America

10 9 8 7 6 5 4 3 2 1

Leisure Press
A Division of Human Kinetics Publishers, Inc.
Box 5076, Champaign, IL 61825-5076
1-800-747-4457

UK Office:
Human Kinetics Publishers (UK) Ltd.
PO Box 18
Rawdon, Leeds LS19 6TG
England
(0532) 504211

Contents

A Word From the USTA

As Director of Coaching for the United States Tennis Association Player Development Program, I applaud your interest in helping young Americans learn the fun and challenging game of tennis. As a tennis coach, you will have the opportunity to introduce a sport to children that they can enjoy for the rest of their lives.

The *Rookie Coaches Tennis Guide* will be an invaluable resource for you. The practical, step-by-step information provided will make you feel well qualified even if you've never coached before. In fact, this guide was designed specifically for novice coaches! All of your concerns have been addressed. You'll understand the importance of your role as a coach; how to communicate effectively with your players; the best way to teach new skills and organize on-court drills; how to promote team spirit; and basic first aid and sport science concepts.

The knowledge you are gaining has an instant application for a new USTA tennis program as well. Coaches such as you are currently introducing thousands of youngsters across the country to **USTA Junior Team Tennis**. This program provides a team opportunity for fun, fitness, and friendship while promoting the philosophy of Fundamentals, Fair & Equal Play, Appropriate Groupings, and Positive Coaching. I encourage all of you to become involved.

On behalf of the United States Tennis Association, I welcome you to coaching and wish you fun and personal fulfillment in your new role.

Stan Smith
USTA Director of Coaching

Welcome to Coaching!

Coaching young people is an exciting way to be involved in tennis. But it isn't easy. The untrained novice coach may be overwhelmed by the responsibilities involved in helping players through their early tennis experiences. Preparing youngsters physically and mentally to compete effectively, fairly, and safely in tennis and providing them a positive role model are among the difficult—but rewarding—tasks you will assume as a coach.

This book will help you meet the challenges and experience the rewards of coaching young players. We call it the *Rookie Coaches Tennis Guide* because it is intended for adults with little or no formal preparation in coaching tennis. In this Rookie Guide you'll learn how to apply general coaching principles and teach tennis-specific rules, skills, and strategies successfully. This book also serves as a text for the American Coaching Effectiveness Program (ACEP) Rookie Course.

We hope you will find coaching rewarding and that you will continue to learn more about coaching and tennis so that you can be the best possible coach for your young players.

If you would like more information about training and materials available for tennis coaches, please contact the USTA at

USTA Junior Team Tennis
707 Alexander Road
Princeton, NJ 08540
(800) 223-0456
In New Jersey: (609) 452-2580

Good coaching!

UNIT 1

Who, Me . . . a Coach?

If you are like most youth league coaches, you were probably recruited from the ranks of concerned parents, tennis enthusiasts, or community volunteers. And, like many rookie *and* veteran coaches, you probably have had little formal instruction on how to coach. But when the call went out for coaches to assist with the area *Junior Team Tennis* program, you answered because you like children and enjoy tennis, and perhaps because you want to be involved in a worthwhile community activity.

I Want to Help, But . . .

Your initial coaching assignment may be difficult. Like many volunteers, you may not know much about the sport you have agreed to coach, or about how to work with children between the ages of 8 and 18. Relax, because this *Rookie Coaches Guide* will help you learn the basics for coaching tennis effectively. In the coming pages you will find the answers to such common questions as these:

- What tools do I need to be a good coach?
- How can I best communicate with my players?
- How do I go about teaching tennis skills?
- What can I do to promote safety?
- What should I do when someone is injured?
- What are the basic rules, skills, and strategies of tennis?
- What practice drills will improve my players' tennis skills?

Before answering these questions, let's take a look at what's involved in being a coach.

Am I a Parent or a Coach?

Many coaches are parents, but the two roles should not be confused. Unlike your role as a parent, as a coach you are responsible not only to yourself and your child, but also to the organization, all the players on the team (including your child), and their parents.

Because of this additional responsibility, your behavior on the court will be different from how you behave at home, and your son or daughter may not understand why. Take the following steps to avoid such problems in coaching your child:

- Ask your child if he or she wants you to coach the team.
- Explain why you wish to be involved with the team.
- Discuss with your son or daughter your new responsibilities and how they will affect your relationship when coaching.
- Limit your ''coach'' behavior to when you are in a coaching role.
- Avoid parenting during practice or game situations, to keep your role clear in your child's mind.
- Reaffirm your love for your child irrespective of his or her performance on the tennis court.

What Are My Responsibilities as a Coach?

A coach assumes the responsibility for doing everything possible to ensure that the youngsters on his or her team will have an enjoyable and safe tennis experience while they learn tennis skills. If you ever doubt your approach, remember ''fun and fundamentals'' are most important.

Provide an Enjoyable Experience

Tennis should be fun. Even if nothing else is accomplished, make certain your players have fun. Take the fun out of tennis and you'll take the kids out of tennis.

Children enter sport for a number of reasons (e.g., to meet and play with other children, to learn skills, and to develop physically), but their major objective is to have fun. Help them satisfy this goal by injecting humor and variety into your practices. Also, make matches nonthreatening, festive experiences for your players. Such an approach will increase your players' desire to participate in the future, which should be the biggest goal of youth sport. Unit 2 will help you learn how to satisfy your player's yearning for fun and keep winning in perspective. And unit 3 will describe how to communicate this perspective effectively to them.

Provide a Safe Experience

You are responsible for planning and teaching activities in such a way that the progression between activities minimizes risks (see units 4 and 5). Further, you must ensure that the courts on which your team practices and plays, and the equipment team members use, are free of hazards. Finally, you need to protect yourself from any legal liability that might arise from your involvement as a coach. Unit 5 will help you take the appropriate precautions.

Teach Basic Tennis Skills

In becoming a coach, you take on the role of educator. You must teach your players the fundamental skills and strategies necessary for success in tennis. That means that you need to "go to school." If you don't know the basics of tennis now, you can learn them by reading the second half of this manual. But even if you know tennis as a player, do you know how to teach it? This book will help you get started.

You'll also find it easier to provide good educational experiences for your players if you plan your practices. Unit 4 provides some guidelines for effective planning of practices, and unit 7 contains a step-by-step description of 12 practice sessions (marked by color on the edge of the pages).

Getting Help

Veteran coaches in your league are an especially good source of help for you. So are local tennis teaching professionals. They have all experienced the same emotions and concerns you are facing, and their advice can be invaluable as you work through your first season.

You can get additional help by watching tennis coaches in practices and games, attending workshops, reading tennis publications, and studying instructional videos. In addition to the United States Tennis Association, the following national organizations will assist you in obtaining more tennis coaching information:

American Coaching Effectiveness
  Program
Box 5076
Champaign, IL 61825-5076
(800) 747-4457

United States Professional Tennis
  Association
World Headquarters
One USPTA Centre
3535 Briarpark Drive
Houston, TX 77042
(713) 97-USPTA

United States Professional Tennis
  Registry
P.O. Box 4739
Hilton Head Island, SC 29938
(800) 421-6289
In South Carolina: (803) 785-7244

Coaching tennis is a rewarding experience. Just as you want your players to be the best they can be, learn all you can about coaching so you can be the best tennis coach you can be.

UNIT 2

What Tools Do I Need to Coach?

TOOL BOX

Have you purchased the traditional coaching tools—things like a whistle, bucket of balls, tennis shoes, and a clipboard? They'll help you coach, but to be a successful coach you'll need five other tools that cannot be bought. These tools are available only through self-examination and hard work; they're easy to remember with the acronym COACH:

C—Comprehension

O—Outlook

A—Affection

C—Character

H—Humor

Comprehension

Comprehension of the rules, skills, and tactics of tennis is required. It is essential that you understand the basic elements of tennis. To assist you in learning about the game, the second half of this guide describes rules, skills, and tactics and suggests how to plan for the season and individual practices. In the tennis-specific section of this guide, you'll also find a variety of drills to use in developing tennis skills (see the pages in unit 7 with blue-colored edges).

To improve your comprehension of tennis, take the following steps:

- Read the tennis-specific section of this book.
- Refer to other tennis coaching books.
- Contact any of the organizations listed on page 3.
- Talk with other, more experienced tennis coaches.
- Observe local college, high school, and other *Junior Team Tennis* matches.
- Watch tennis matches on television.
- Attend a *USTA Junior Team Tennis* Coaches Workshop.

In addition to having tennis knowledge, you must implement proper training and safety methods so your players can participate with little risk of injury. Even then, tennis injuries will occur. And more often than not, you'll be the first person responding to your players' injuries, so be sure you understand the basic emergency care procedures described in unit 5. Also read in that unit how to handle more serious tennis injury situations.

Outlook

This coaching tool refers to your perspective and goals—what you are seeking as a coach. The most common coaching objectives are (a) to have fun, (b) to help players develop their physical, mental, and social skills, and (c) to win. Thus *Outlook* involves the priorities you set, your planning, and your vision for the future.

To work successfully with children in a tennis setting, you must have your priorities in order. In just what order do you rank the importance of fun, development, and winning?

Answer the following questions to examine your objectives.

Of which situation would you be most proud?

a. Knowing that each participant enjoyed playing tennis.
b. Seeing that all players improved their tennis skills.
c. Winning the league championship.

Which statement best reflects your thoughts about tennis?

a. If it isn't fun, don't do it.
b. Everyone should learn something every day.
c. Tennis isn't fun if you don't win.

How would you like your players to remember you?

a. As a coach who was fun to play for.

b. As a coach who provided a good base of fundamental skills.

c. As a coach who had a winning record.

Which would you most like to hear a parent of a child on your team say?

a. Billy really had a good time playing tennis this year.

b. Susie learned some important lessons playing tennis this year.

c. Ronnie played on the first-place tennis team this year.

Which of the following would be the most rewarding moment of your season?

a. Having your team not want to stop playing even after practice is over.

b. Seeing one of your players finally master the skill of a backhand groundstroke.

c. Winning the league championship.

Look over your answers. If you most often selected "a" responses, then having fun is more important to you. A majority of "b" answers suggests that skill development is what attracts you to coaching. And if "c" was your most frequent response, winning is tops on your list of coaching priorities.

Most coaches say fun and development are more important, but when actually coaching, some coaches emphasize—indeed overemphasize—winning. You too will face situations that challenge you to keep winning in its proper perspective. During such moments you'll have to choose between emphasizing your players' development or winning. If your priorities are in order, your players' well-being will take precedence over your team's win-loss record every time.

Take the following actions to better define your outlook:

1. Determine your priorities for the season.

2. Prepare for situations that challenge your priorities.

3. Set goals for yourself and your players that are consistent with those priorities.

4. Plan how you and your players can best attain those goals.

5. Review your goals frequently to be sure that you are staying on track.

It is particularly important for coaches to permit all young players to participate. Each youngster should have an opportunity to develop skills and have fun—even if it means sacrificing a win or two during the season. After all, wouldn't you prefer losing a couple of games to losing a couple of players' interest in tennis?

Remember that the challenge and joy of tennis is experienced through *striving to win*, not through winning itself. Players who aren't allowed to play are denied the opportunity to strive to win. And herein lies the irony: A coach who allows all of his or her players to participate will—in the end—come out on top.

ACEP has a motto that will help you keep your outlook in the best interest of the kids on your team. It summarizes in four words all you need to remember when establishing your coaching priorities:

Athletes First, Winning Second

This motto recognizes that striving to win is an important, even vital, part of tennis. But it emphatically states that no efforts in striving to win should be made at the expense of players' well-being, development, and enjoyment.

Affection

This is another vital *tool* you will want to have in your coaching kit: a genuine concern for the young people you coach. Affection involves having a love for children, a desire to share with them your love and knowledge of tennis, and the patience and understanding that allows each individual playing for you to grow from his or her involvement in tennis.

Successful coaches have a real concern for the health and welfare of their players. They care that each child on the team has an

enjoyable and successful experience. They have a strong desire to work with children and be involved in their growth. And they have the patience to work with those who are slower to learn or less capable of performing. If you have such qualities or are willing to work hard to develop them, then you have the *affection* necessary to coach young players.

There are many ways to demonstrate your affection and patience, including these:

- Make an effort to get to know each player on your team.
- Treat each player as an individual.
- Empathize with players' trying to learn new and difficult tennis skills.
- Treat players as you would like to be treated under similar circumstances.
- Be in control of your emotions.
- Show your enthusiasm for being involved with your team.
- Keep an upbeat and positive tone in all of your communications.

Character

Youngsters learn by listening to what adults say. But they learn even more by watching the behavior of certain important individuals. As a coach, you are likely to be a significant figure in the lives of your players. Will you be a good role model?

Having good *character* means modeling appropriate behaviors for tennis and life. That means more than just saying the right things. It also means doing the right thing. The "Do as I say, not as I do" approach won't work in coaching. Be in control before, during, and after all matches and practices. And don't be afraid to admit that you were wrong. No one is perfect!

Consider the following steps to being a good role model:

- Take stock of your strengths and weaknesses.
- Build on your strengths.
- Set goals for yourself to improve upon those areas you would not like to see mimicked.
- If you slip up apologize to your team and to yourself. You'll do better next time.

Humor

Humor is often overlooked as a coaching tool. For our use it means having the ability to laugh *at* yourself and *with* your players during practices and matches. Nothing helps balance the tone of a serious, skill-learning session like a chuckle or two. And

a sense of humor puts in perspective the many mistakes your young players will make. So don't get upset over each miscue or respond negatively to erring players. Allow your players and yourself to enjoy the "ups" and don't dwell on the "downs."

Here are some tips for injecting humor into your practices:

- Make practices fun by including a variety of activities.
- Keep all players involved in drills and practice matches.

- Consider laughter by your players a sign of enjoyment, not waning discipline.
- Smile!

Where Do You Stand?

To take stock of your "coaching tool kit," rank yourself on the three questions for each of the five coaching tools. Simply circle the number that best describes your *present* status on each item.

Not at all		Somewhat		Very much so
1	2	3	4	5

Comprehension

1. Could you explain the rules of tennis to other parents without studying for a long time?　　1 2 3 4 5
2. Do you know how to organize and conduct safe tennis practices?　　1 2 3 4 5
3. Do you know how to provide first aid for most common, minor sport injuries?　　1 2 3 4 5

Comprehension Score: _____

Outlook

4. Do you have winning in its proper perspective when you coach?　　1 2 3 4 5
5. Do you plan for every meeting, practice, and match?　　1 2 3 4 5
6. Do you have a vision of what you want your players to be able to do by the end of the season?　　1 2 3 4 5

Outlook Score: _____

Affection

7. Do you enjoy working with children?　　1 2 3 4 5
8. Are you patient with youngsters learning new skills?　　1 2 3 4 5
9. Are you able to show your players that you care?　　1 2 3 4 5

Affection Score: _____

Character

10. Are your words and behaviors consistent with each other?　　1 2 3 4 5
11. Are you a good model for your players?　　1 2 3 4 5
12. Do you keep negative emotions under control before, during, and after matches?　　1 2 3 4 5

Character Score: _____

Not at all		Somewhat		Very much so
1	2	3	4	5

Humor

13. Do you usually smile at your players?   1   2   3   4   5

14. Are your practices fun?   1   2   3   4   5

15. Are you able to laugh at your mistakes?   1   2   3   4   5

Humor Score: _____

If you scored 9 or less on any of the coaching tools, be sure to reread those sections of the unit carefully. And even if you scored 15 on each tool, don't be complacent. Keep learning! Then you'll be well-equipped with the tools you need to coach young athletes.

UNIT 3

How Should I Communicate With My Players?

EVERYBODY GOT THAT?

ow you know the tools needed to COACH: Comprehension, Outlook, Affection, Character, and Humor are essential for effective coaching. Without them, you'd have a difficult time getting started.

But none of these tools will work if you don't know how to use them with your players—that requires skillful communication. This unit examines what communication is and how you can become a more effective communicator-coach.

What's Involved in Communication?

Coaches often believe that communication involves only instructing players to do something, but verbal commands are a very small part of the communication process. More than half of what is communicated is nonverbal. So remember when you are coaching, "Actions speak louder than words."

Communication in its simplest form involves two people: a sender and a receiver. The sender can transmit the message verbally, through facial expression, and through body language. Once the message is sent, the receiver must try to determine the meaning of the message. A receiver who fails to attend or listen will miss part, if not all, of the message.

How Can I Send More Effective Messages?

Young players often have little understanding of the rules and skills of tennis and probably even less confidence in playing it. So they need accurate, understandable, and supportive messages to help them along. That's why your verbal and nonverbal messages are so important.

Verbal Messages

"Sticks and stones may break my bones, but words will never hurt me" isn't true. Spoken words can have a strong and long-lasting effect. And coaches' words are particularly influential, because youngsters place great importance on what coaches say. Therefore, whether you are correcting misbehavior, teaching a player how to hit a forehand, or praising a player for good effort, be positive, but honest; state it clearly and simply; say it loud enough, and say it again; and be consistent.

Be Positive, but Honest

Nothing turns people off like hearing someone nag all the time. Young players are similarly discouraged by a coach who gripes

constantly. The kids on your team need encouragement because many of them probably doubt their ability to play tennis. So look for and tell your players what they did well.

On the other hand, kids know all too well when they've erred, and no cheerfully expressed cliche can undo their mistakes. If you fail to acknowledge your players' errors, they'll think you are a phony.

A good way to handle situations in which you have identified and must correct improper technique is to serve your players a "compliment sandwich."

1. Point out what the athlete did correctly.
2. Let the player know what was incorrect in the performance and instruct him or her how to correct it.
3. Encourage the player by reemphasizing what he or she did well.

State It Clearly and Simply

Positive and honest messages are good, but only if expressed directly and in words your players understand. "Beating around the bush" is ineffective and inefficient. If you do ramble, your players will miss the point of your message and probably lose interest. Here are some tips for saying things clearly.

- Organize your thoughts before speaking to your players.
- Explain things thoroughly, but don't bore them with long-winded monologues.
- Use language your players can understand. However, avoid trying to be "hip" by using their age group's slang vocabulary.

Say It Loud Enough, and Say It Again

Talk to your team in a voice that all members can hear and interpret. A crisp, vigorous voice commands attention and respect; garbled and weak speech is tuned out. It's ok, in fact appropriate, to soften your voice when speaking to a player individually about a personal problem. But most of the time your messages will be for all your players to hear, so make sure they can! A word of caution, however: Don't dominate the setting with a booming voice that detracts attention from players' performances.

Sometimes what you say, even if stated loud and clear, won't sink in the first time. This may be particularly true with young players hearing words they don't understand. To avoid boring repetition and yet still get your message across, say the same thing in a slightly different way. For instance, you

might first tell your players, "Risk only one line on the approach shot." Soon afterward remind them to "Make sure your target on the approach shot is well inside the sideline but deep near the baseline." The second form of the message may get through to players who missed it the first time around.

Send Consistent Messages

People often say things in ways that imply a different message. For example, a touch of sarcasm added to the words "way to go" sends an entirely different message than the words themselves suggest. It is essential that you avoid sending such mixed messages. Keep the tone of your voice consistent with the words you use. And don't say something one day and contradict it the next; players will get confused.

Nonverbal Messages

Just as you should be consistent in the tone of voice and words you use, you should also keep your verbal and nonverbal messages consistent. An extreme example of failing to do this would be shaking your head, indicating disapproval, while at the same time telling a player "nice try." Which is the player to believe, your gesture or your words?

Messages can be sent nonverbally in a number of ways. Facial expressions and body language are just two of the more obvious forms of nonverbal signals that can help you when you coach.

Facial Expressions

The look on a person's face is the quickest clue to what he or she thinks or feels. Your players know this, so they will study your face, looking for any sign that will tell them more than words you say. Don't try to fool them by putting on a happy or blank "mask." They'll see through it, and you'll lose credibility.

Serious, stone-faced expressions are no help to kids who need cues as to how they are performing. They will just assume you're unhappy or disinterested. So don't be afraid to smile. A smile from a coach can give a great boost to an unsure young athlete. Plus, a smile lets your players know that you are happy coaching them. But don't overdo it, or your players won't be able to tell when you are genuinely pleased by something they've done or when you are just "putting on" a smiling face.

Body Language

How would your players think you felt if you came to practice slouched over, with head down and shoulders slumped? Tired? Bored? Unhappy? How would they think you felt if you watched them during a contest with your hands on your hips, your jaws clenched, and your face reddened? Upset with them? Disgusted at an official? Mad at a fan? Probably some or all of these things would enter your players' minds. That's why you should carry yourself in a pleasant, confident, and vigorous manner. Such a posture not only projects happiness with your coaching role but also provides a good example for your young players who may model your behavior.

Physical contact can also be a very important use of body language. A handshake, a pat on the head, an arm around the shoulder, or even a big hug are effective ways of showing approval, concern, affection, and

joy to your players. Youngsters are especially in need of this type of nonverbal message. Keep within the obvious moral and legal limits, but don't be reluctant to touch your players and send a message that can only truly be expressed in that way.

How Can I Improve My Receiving Skills?

Now let's examine the other half of the communication process—receiving messages. Too often people are very good senders but very poor receivers of messages. As a coach of young players it is essential that you are able to fulfill both roles effectively.

The requirements for receiving messages are quite simple, but people seem to naturally enjoy hearing themselves talk more than listening to others. You can be a better receiver of your players' messages if you are willing to read about the keys to receiving messages and then make a strong effort to use them with your players. You'll be surprised what you've been missing.

Attention!

First you must pay attention; you must want to hear what others have to communicate to you. That's not always easy when you're busy coaching and have many things competing for your attention. But in one-to-one or team meetings with players, you must really focus on what they are telling you, both verbally and nonverbally. Not only will such focused attention help you catch every word your players say, but you'll also notice your players' moods and physical states, and you'll get an idea of your players' feelings toward you and other players on the team.

Listen CARE-FULLy

How we receive messages from others, perhaps more than anything else we do, demonstrates how much we care for the sender and what that person has to tell us. If you care little for your players or have little regard for what they have to say, it will show in how you attend and listen to them. Check yourself. Do you find your mind wandering to what you are going to do after practice while one of your players is talking to you? Do you frequently have to ask your players, "What did you say?" If so, you need to work on your receiving mechanics of attending and listening. If you find that you're missing the messages your players send, perhaps the most critical question you should ask yourself is this: Do I care?

How Do I Put It All Together?

So far we've discussed separately the sending and receiving of messages. But we all know that senders and receivers switch roles several times during an interaction. One person initiates a communication by sending a message to another person who then receives the message. The receiver then switches roles and becomes the sender by responding to the person who sent the initial message. These verbal and nonverbal responses are called *feedback*.

Your players will be looking to you for feedback all the time. They will want to know how you think they are performing, what you think of their ideas, and whether

their efforts please you. How you respond will strongly affect your players. So let's take a look at a few general types of feedback and examine their possible effects.

Providing Instructions

With young players, much of your feedback will involve answering questions about how to play tennis. Your instructive responses to these questions should include both verbal and nonverbal instructional feedback. Here are some suggestions for giving instructional feedback:

- Keep verbal instructions simple and concise.
- Use demonstrations to provide nonverbal instructional feedback (see unit 4).
- "Walk" players through the skill, or use a slow-motion demonstration if they are having trouble learning.

Correcting Errors

When your players perform incorrectly, you need to provide informative feedback to correct the error—and the sooner the better. And when you do correct errors, keep in mind these two principles: Use negative criticism sparingly, and keep calm.

Use Negative Criticism Sparingly

Although you may need to punish players for horseplay or dangerous activities by scolding them or temporarily removing them from activity, avoid reprimanding players for performance errors. Admonishing players for honest mistakes makes them afraid to even try. And nothing ruins a youngster's enjoyment of tennis more than a coach who harps on every miscue. So instead, correct your players by using the positive approach. Your players will enjoy playing more, and you'll enjoy coaching more.

Keep Calm

Don't fly off the handle when your players make mistakes. Remember, you're coaching young and inexperienced players, not pros. You'll therefore see more incorrect than

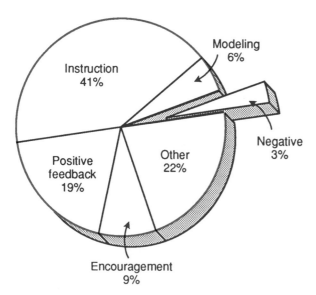

Coaches, Be Positive!
Only a very small percentage of ACEP-trained coaches' behaviors are negative.

Instruction 41%
Modeling 6%
Negative 3%
Other 22%
Positive feedback 19%
Encouragement 9%

correct techniques, and you'll probably have more discipline problems than you expect. But throwing a tantrum over each error or misbehavior will only inhibit your players or suggest to them the wrong kind of behavior to model. So let your players know that mistakes aren't the end of the world; stay cool!

Positive Feedback

Praising players when they have performed or behaved well is an effective way of getting them to repeat (or try to repeat) that behavior in the future. And positive feedback for effort is an especially effective way to motivate youngsters to work on difficult skills. So rather than shouting and providing negative feedback to a player who has made a mistake, try offering players a compliment sandwich, described on page 12.

Sometimes just the way you word feedback can make it more positive than negative. For example, instead of saying, "Don't take such a big swing on the volley," you might say, "Shorten your swing by blocking the ball and you'll have even more success." Then your players will be focusing on what to do instead of what not to do.

You can give positive feedback verbally and nonverbally. Telling a player, especially

in front of teammates, that he or she has performed well is a great way to boost the confidence of a youngster. And a pat on the back or a handshake can be a very tangible way of communicating your recognition of a player's performance.

Whom Else Do I Need to Communicate With?

Coaching involves not only sending and receiving messages and providing proper feedback to players, but also interacting with parents, fans, game officials, and opposing coaches. So try the following suggestions for communicating with these groups.

Parents

A player's parents need to be assured that their son or daughter is under the direction of a coach who is both knowledgeable about tennis and concerned about the youngster's well-being. You can put their worries to rest by holding a preseason parent orientation meeting in which you describe your background and your approach to coaching.

If parents contact you with a concern during the season, listen to them closely and try to offer positive responses. If you need to communicate with parents, catch them after a practice, give them a phone call, or send a note through the mail. Messages sent to parents through children are too often lost, misinterpreted, or forgotten.

Fans

The stands probably won't be overflowing at your matches, but that only means that you'll more easily hear the few fans who criticize your coaching. When you hear something negative said about the job you're doing, don't respond. Keep calm, consider whether the message had any value, and if not, forget it. The best approach is to put away your "rabbit ears" and communicate to fans through your actions that you are a confident, competent coach.

Game Officials

How you communicate with officials will have a great influence on the way your

players behave toward them, so you need to set an example. Greet officials with a handshake, an introduction, and perhaps some casual conversation about the upcoming contest. Indicate your respect for them before, during, and after the contest. Don't make nasty remarks, shout, or use disrespectful body gestures. Your players will see you do it, and they'll get the idea that such behavior is appropriate. Plus, if the official hears or sees you, the communication between the two of you will break down.

Opposing Coaches

Make an effort to visit with the coach of the opposing team before the match. During the match, don't get into a personal feud with the opposing coach. Remember, it's the kids, not the coaches, who are competing. And by getting along well with the opposing coach you'll show your players that competition involves cooperation.

Summary Checklist

Now, check your coach-communication skills by answering "Yes" or "No" to the following questions.

	Yes	No
1. Are your verbal messages to your players positive and honest?	___	___
2. Do you speak loudly, clearly, and in a language your players understand?	___	___
3. Do you remember to repeat instructions to your players, in case they didn't hear you the first time?	___	___
4. Are your tone of voice and your nonverbal messages consistent with the words you use?	___	___
5. Do your facial expressions and body language express interest in and happiness with your coaching role?	___	___
6. Are you attentive to your players and able to pick up even their small verbal and nonverbal cues?	___	___
7. Do you really care about what your players say to you?	___	___
8. Do you instruct rather than criticize when your players make errors?	___	___
9. Are you usually positive when responding to things your players say and do?	___	___

10. Do you try to communicate in a cooperative and respectful manner with
    players' parents, fans, game officials, and opposing coaches?   ____ ____

   If you answered "No" to any of these questions, you may want to refer back to the section
of the chapter where the topic was discussed. Now is the time to address communication
problems, not when you're coaching your players.

UNIT 4

How Do I Get My Team Ready to Play?

To coach tennis, you must understand the basic rules, skills, and strategies of the game. The second part of this guide provides the basic information you'll need to Comprehend the sport of tennis.

But all the tennis knowledge in the world will do you little good unless you present it effectively to your players. That's why this unit is so important. Here you will learn the steps to take when teaching tennis skills, as well as practical guidelines for planning your season and individual practices.

How Do I Teach Tennis Skills?

Many people believe that the only qualification needed to coach is to have played the sport. It's helpful to have played, but there is much more to coaching successfully. And even if you haven't played tennis, you can still learn to coach successfully with this IDEA:

I —Introduce the skill.

D—Demonstrate the skill.

E—Explain the skill.

A—Attend to players practicing the skill.

Introduce the Skill

Players, especially young and inexperienced ones, need to know what skill they are learning and why they are learning it. You should therefore take these three steps every time you introduce a skill to your players:

1. Get your players' attention.
2. Name the skill.
3. Explain the importance of the skill.

Get Your Players' Attention

Because youngsters are easily distracted, use some method to get their attention. Some coaches use interesting news items or stories. Others use jokes. And others simply project an enthusiasm that gets their players to listen. Whatever method you use, speak slightly above the normal volume and look your players in the eye when you speak. Also, arrange the players in two or three evenly spaced rows, facing you and not the sun or some source of distraction. Then ask if all can see you before you begin.

Name the Skill

Although you might mention other common names for the skill, decide which one you'll use and stick with it. This will help avoid confusion and enhance communication among your players.

Explain the Importance of the Skill

Although the importance of a skill may be apparent to you, your players may be less able to see how the skill will help them become better tennis players. Offer them a reason for learning the skill and describe how the skill relates to more advanced skills.

The most difficult aspect of coaching is this: Coaches must learn to let athletes learn. Tennis skills should be taught so they have meaning to the child, not just meaning to the coach.

Rainer Martens, ACEP Founder

Demonstrate the Skill

The demonstration step is the most important part of teaching tennis skills to young players who may have never done anything closely resembling the skill. They need a picture, not just words. They need to see how the skill is performed.

If you are unable to perform the skill correctly, have an assistant coach or someone skilled in tennis perform the demonstration. These tips will help make your demonstrations more effective.

- Use correct form.
- Demonstrate the skill several times.
- Slow down the action, if possible, during one or two performances so players can see every movement involved in the skill.
- Perform the skill at different angles so your players can get a "full perspective" of it.
- Demonstrate the skill with both the right and the left hand.

Explain the Skill

Players learn more effectively when they're given a brief explanation of the skill along with the demonstration. Use simple terms and, if possible, relate the skill to previously learned skills. Ask your players whether

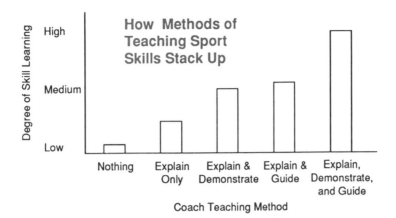

they understand your description. If someone looks confused, have him or her explain the skill back to you.

Complex skills often are better understood when they are explained in more manageable parts. For instance, if you want to teach your players how to hit a full-swing serve, you might take the following steps:

1. Show them a correct performance of the entire skill, and explain its function in tennis.
2. Break down the skill and point out its component parts to your players.
3. Have players perform each of the component skills you have already taught them, such as stance, grip, backswing and toss, contact, and follow-through.
4. After players have demonstrated their ability to perform the separate parts of the skill in sequence, reexplain the entire skill.
5. Have players practice the skill.

Attend to Players Practicing the Skill

If the skill you selected was within your players' capabilities and you have done an effective job of introducing, demonstrating, and explaining it, your players should be ready to attempt the skill. Some players may need to be physically guided through the movements during their first few attempts. Walking unsure players through the skill in

this way will help them gain confidence to perform the skill on their own.

Your teaching duties don't end when all your players have demonstrated that they understand how to perform the skill. In fact, a significant part of your teaching will involve observing closely the hit-and-miss trial performances of your players.

As you observe players' efforts in drills and activities, offer positive, corrective feedback in the form of the "compliment sandwich" described in unit 3. If a player performs the skill properly, acknowledge it and offer praise. Keep in mind that your feedback will have a great influence on your players' motivation to practice and improve their performance.

Remember too that young players need individual instruction. So set aside a time before, during, or after a practice to give individual help.

What Planning Do I Need to Do?

Beginning coaches often make the mistake of showing up for the first practice with no particular plan in mind. These coaches find that their practices are unorganized, their players are frustrated and inattentive, and the amount and quality of their skill instruction is limited. Planning is essential to successful teaching and coaching. And it doesn't begin on the way to practice!

Preseason Planning

Effective coaches begin planning well before the start of the season. Among the preseason measures that will make the season more enjoyable, successful, and safe for you and your players are the following:

- Familiarize yourself with *USTA Junior Team Tennis*, especially its philosophy, standards, and area regulations.
- Examine the availability of facilities, equipment, instructional aids, and other materials needed for practices and matches.
- Check to see whether you have liability insurance to cover you when one of your players is hurt (see unit 5). If you don't, get some.
- Establish your coaching priorities regarding having fun, developing players' skills, and winning.
- Select and meet with your assistant coaches to discuss the philosophy, goals, team rules, and plans for the season.
- Register players for the team on the USTA Official Membership Control Sheet/Team Roster. Have them complete player information forms and

obtain medical clearance forms, if required.
- Ask players to provide you with a schedule of known absences or vacations.
- Institute an injury-prevention program for your players.
- Hold a parent orientation meeting to inform parents of your background, philosophy, goals, and instructional approach. Also, give a brief overview of tennis rules, terms, and strategies to familiarize parents or guardians with the sport.

You may be surprised at the number of things you should do even before the first practice. But if you address them during the preseason, the season will be much more enjoyable and productive for you and your players.

In-Season Planning

Your choice of activities during the season should be based on whether they will help your players develop physical and mental skills, knowledge of rules and game tactics, sportsmanship, and a love for the game. All of these goals are important, but we'll focus on the skills and tactics of tennis to give you an idea of how to itemize your objectives.

Goal Setting

What you plan to do during the season must be reasonable for the maturity and skill level of your players. In terms of tennis skills and tactics, you should teach young players the basics and move on to more complex activities only after the players have mastered these easier techniques and strategies.

To begin the season, your instructional goals might include the following:

- Players will be able to hit full-swing serves from the baseline using a proper grip.
- Players will be able to hit a forehand groundstroke with consistency from the baseline.
- Players will be able to hit a backhand groundstroke with consistency from the baseline.

- Players will be able to hit lobs when attacked or out of position.
- Players will be able to hit attacking forehands from the midcourt.
- Players will be able to hit attacking backhands from the midcourt.
- Players will be able to volley effectively at net.
- Players will be able to perform an aggressive overhead smash.
- Players will demonstrate knowledge of tennis rules.
- Players will demonstrate knowledge of basic offensive and defensive strategies in both singles and doubles.

Organizing

After you've defined the skills and tactics you want your players to learn during the season, you can plan how to teach them to your players in practices. But be flexible! If your players are having difficulty learning a skill or tactic, take some extra time until they get the hang of it—even if that means moving back your schedule. After all, if your players are unable to perform the fundamental skills, they'll never execute the more complex skills you have scheduled for them.

Still, it helps to have a plan for progressing players through skills during the season. A season plan of 12 practices is provided in unit 7 to show how to schedule your skill instruction in an organized and progressive manner. If this is your first coaching experience, you may wish to follow the plan as it stands. If you have some previous experience, you may want to modify the schedule to better fit the needs of your team.

What Makes Up a Good Practice?

A good instructional plan makes practice preparation much easier. Have players work on more important and less difficult goals in early season practice sessions. And see to it that players master basic skills before moving on to more advanced ones.

It is helpful to establish one objective for each practice: But try to include a variety of activities related to that objective. For example, although your primary objective might be to improve players' volleying skills, you should have players perform several different drills designed to enhance that single skill. To add more variety to your practices, vary the order of the activities.

In general, we recommend that each of your practices include these components:

- Warm-up
- Practice previously taught skills
- Teach and practice new skills
- Practice under matchlike conditions
- Cool-down
- Evaluation

Warm-Up

Check the fit and suitability of the equipment used by your players. Worn or improperly sized racket grips can cause a variety of injuries, both minor and serious. Players must wear sneakers for tennis. Other types of shoes provide inadequate traction and may wear out quickly, hurt players' feet, or damage the court.

Practice Previously Taught Skills

Devote part of each practice to having players work on the fundamental skills they already know. But remember, kids like variety. So organize and modify drills to keep everyone involved and interested. Praise and encourage players when you notice improvement, and offer individual assistance to those who need help.

Teach and Practice New Skills

Gradually build on your players' existing skills by giving players something new to practice each session. The proper method for teaching tennis skills is described in unit 7. Refer to that section if you have any questions about teaching new skills or if you want to evaluate your teaching approach periodically during the season.

Practice Under Competitive Conditions

Competition among teammates during practices prepares players for actual games and informs young players about their abilities relative to their peers. Youngsters also seem to have more fun in competitive activities.

You can create contestlike conditions by using competitive drills, modified games, and practice matches (see unit 7). However, consider the following guidelines before introducing competition into your practices.

- Provide all players an equal opportunity to participate.
- Match players by ability and physical maturity.
- Make certain players can execute fundamental skills before they compete in groups.

- Emphasize performing well, not winning, in every competition.
- Give players room to make mistakes by avoiding constant evaluation of their performances.

Cool-Down

Each practice should wind down with a 5- to 10-minute period of light exercise, including jogging, performance of simple skills, and some stretching. The cool-down allows players' bodies to return to the resting state and avoid stiffness, and it affords you an opportunity to review the practice.

Evaluation

At the end of practice spend a few minutes with your players reviewing how well the session accomplished the objective you had set. Even if your evaluation is negative, show optimism for future practices and send players off on an upbeat note.

How Do I Put a Practice Together?

Simply knowing the six practice components is not enough. You must also be able to arrange those components into a logical progression and fit them into a time schedule. Now, using your instructional goals as a guide for selecting what skills to have your players work on, try to plan a tennis practice you might conduct. The following example should help you get started.

Sample Practice Plan

Performance Objective: Players will be able to hit full-swing serves from the baseline.

Component	Time	Activity or drill
Warm-up	8 min	Groundstroke & Dig followed by selected stretches
Teach	12 min	Serve Progression

Component	Time	Activity or drill
Practice previously learned skills	20 min	Serve Practice, Serve and Return
Play under matchlike conditions	10 min	Team Singles
Evaluation and cool-down	10 min	Ball Reaction drill, stretching

Summary Checklist

During your tennis season, check your teaching and planning skills periodically. As you gain more coaching experience, you should be able to answer "Yes" to each of the following.

When you teach tennis skills to your players, do you

— arrange the players so all can see and hear?

— introduce the skill clearly and explain its importance?

— demonstrate the skill properly several times?

— explain the skill simply and accurately?

— attend closely to players practicing the skill?

— offer corrective, positive feedback or praise after observing players' attempts at the skill?

When you plan, do you remember to plan for

— preseason events like player registration, liability protection, use of facilities, and parent orientation?

— season goals such as the development of players' physical skills, mental skills, sportsmanship, and enjoyment?

— practice components such as warm-up, practicing previously taught skills, teaching and practicing new skills, practicing under gamelike conditions, cool-down, and evaluation?

UNIT 5

What About Safety?

One of your players is running wide to hit a passing shot and steps on a ball from the next court, causing the player to fall. You notice that your player is not getting up from the court and seems to be in pain. What do you do?

ne of the least pleasant aspects of coaching is seeing players get hurt. Fortunately there are many preventive measures coaches can institute to reduce the risk. But in spite of such efforts, injury remains a reality of tennis participation; consequently, you must be prepared to provide first aid when injuries occur and to protect yourself against unjustified lawsuits. This unit will describe how you can

- create the safest possible environment for your players,

- provide emergency first aid to players when they get hurt, and
- protect yourself from injury liability.

How Do I Keep My Players From Getting Hurt?

Injuries may occur because of poor preventive measures. Part of your planning, described in unit 4, should include steps that give your players the best possible chance for injury-free participation. These steps include the following:

- Preseason physical examination
- Physical conditioning
- Equipment and facilities inspection
- Matching players by physical maturity and warning of inherent risks
- Proper supervision and record keeping
- Sufficient hydration
- Warm-up and cool-down

Preseason Physical Examination

In the absence of severe injury or ongoing illness, your players should have physical examinations every 2 years. If a player has a known complication, a physician's consent should be obtained before participation is allowed. You should also have a player's parents or guardians sign a participation agreement form and a release form to allow their son or daughter to be treated in the case of an emergency.

Physical Conditioning

Muscles, tendons, and ligaments unaccustomed to vigorous and long-lasting physical activity are prone to injury. Therefore, prepare your players to withstand the exertion of playing tennis. An effective conditioning program for tennis would involve sprinting and other forms of explosive movement.

Make conditioning drills and activities fun. Include a skill component, like running and hitting, to prevent players from becoming bored or looking upon the activity as "work."

Equipment and Facilities Inspection

Check the fit and suitability of the equipment used by your players. Worn or improperly sized racket grips can cause a variety of injuries, both minor and serious. Players must wear sneakers for tennis. Other types of shoes provide inadequate traction and may wear out quickly, hurt players' feet, or damage the court.

Examine regularly the court on which your players practice and play. Remove hazards, report conditions you cannot remedy, and request maintenance as necessary.

Matching Players by Maturity and Warning of Inherent Risks

Children of the same age can differ in height and weight by 6 inches and 50 pounds. That's why in tennis, where larger youngsters may hit the ball much harder, it's essential to match players against opponents of similar size and physical maturity. Such an approach gives smaller, less mature children a better chance to succeed and avoid injury and provides larger children with more of a challenge.

Matching helps protect you from certain liability concerns. But you also must warn players of the inherent risks involved in

playing tennis, because "failure to warn" is one of the most convincing arguments used in lawsuits against coaches. So thoroughly explain the inherent risks of tennis, and make sure each player knows, understands, and appreciates those risks.

Liability Waivers

The preseason parent-orientation meeting is a good opportunity to explain the risks of tennis to parents and players. It is also a good occasion on which to have both the players and their parents sign waivers releasing you from liability should an injury occur. Such waivers do not relieve you of responsibility for your players' well-being, but they are recommended by lawyers.

Proper Supervision and Record Keeping

With youngsters, your mere presence in the area of play is not enough; you must actively plan and direct team activities and closely observe and evaluate players' participation. You're the watchdog responsible for the players' well-being. So if you notice a player limping or grimacing, give him or her a rest and examine the extent of the injury.

As a coach, you're also required to enforce the rules of tennis, prohibit dangerous horse-play, and hold practices only under safe weather conditions. These specific supervisory activities will make the play environment more safe for your players and will help protect you from liability if a mishap does occur.

For further protection, keep records of your season plans, practice plans, and players' injuries. Season and practice plans come in handy when you need evidence that players have been taught certain skills, whereas emergency treatment forms and accurate, detailed accident report forms offer protection against unfounded lawsuits. Ask for these forms from the league to which you belong. And hold onto these records for several years so that an "old tennis injury" of a former player doesn't come back to haunt you.

Sufficient Hydration

The most common danger for tennis players is dehydration—the loss of body fluids through sweating that can result in cramps, heat exhaustion, or worse. Water should be available for players to drink before, during, and after play. If players wait until they are thirsty to drink, they have already waited too long. So encourage players to take frequent water breaks to maintain proper hydration.

EMERGENCY TREATMENT FORM

TO WHOM IT MAY CONCERN:
As a parent and/or guardian of _____, a minor, I herewith authorize treatment by a qualified and licenced medical doctor in the event of a medical emergency which, in the opinion of the attending physician, may endanger his or her life, cause disfigurement, physical impairment, or undue discomfort if delayed. This authority is granted only after a reasonable effort has been made to reach me.

Name of Parent/Guardian _____

Address _____ Phone _____

Family Physician _____ Phone _____

Dates during which release is granted: From: _____ To: _____

Specific medical allergies, chronic illness or other medical conditions staff should be aware of: _____
_____

Other contact in case of emergency: Name _____ Relationship _____ Phone _____

This release form is completed and signed of my own free will with the sole purpose of authorizing medical treatment under emergency circumstances in my absence.

Signature _____ Notarized by: _____
Father, Mother, or Legal Guardian   Date: _____

Printed with the permission of the Rutgers Youth Sports Research Council.

Warm-Up and Cool-Down

Although young bodies are generally very limber, they too can get tight from inactivity. Therefore, a warm-up period of approximately 10 minutes before each practice is strongly recommended. Warm-up should address each muscle group and get the heart rate elevated in preparation for strenuous activity. Easy running followed by these stretching exercises is a common sequence (hold each stretch for 20 seconds, then release):

Hamstring Stretch—Lie supine (on back) with knees bent and feet flat on the court. Straighten the exercise knee, bringing the leg toward the trunk. Gently pull with both hands to give extra stretch, as shown in Figure 5.1. Bring toes toward the face to stretch calf muscles. Repeat the stretch with the opposite leg.

Figure 5.1 Hamstring stretch.

Hip Twist—Lie supine (on back) with knees bent, feet flat on the court, hands clasped behind the head, and arms resting on the court. Place the left ankle outside the right knee. Use the left leg to pull the right knee toward the floor, as shown in Figure 5.2. Keep the upper back, head, shoulders, and elbows flat on the court. Move slowly and absolutely *do not* rock side to side. Switch legs and repeat the stretch.

Figure 5.2 Hip twist.

Long Sitting Stretch—Sit on the court with both legs straight, toes pointing toward your face, and hands resting on the thighs. Lean forward over both legs, bringing the chest toward the thighs, as shown in Figure 5.3. Keep looking straight ahead but do not reach for the toes.

Figure 5.3 Long-sitting stretch.

Groin Stretch—Stand with legs as far apart as possible without being painful and keep abdominal muscles firm. Place the left hand on the left knee and the right hand on the right hip. Slowly bend the left knee until the right thigh is nearly parallel to the court (Figure 5.4). Roll onto the inner side of the right foot while keeping the foot on the floor during the stretch. Repeat the stretch in the opposite direction.

Figure 5.4 Groin stretch.

Stork Stretch—Stand on the left leg, holding onto the fence or net with the left hand for balance. Bend the right knee and grasp the right ankle with the right hand (knee will be pointing forward). Roll the pelvis under so that the back is flat. Keeping the lower back flat and buttocks tucked under, bring the right knee down as far as possible, trying to point the knee straight down to the court, as shown in Figure 5.5.

Figure 5.5 Stork stretch.

Fence Stretch—Stand facing the fence with the left leg behind the right. Place both hands against the fence for balance, as shown in Figure 5.6a. Keep the body in a straight line throughout the exercise, and do not let the left foot rotate outward. Holding the left knee straight and keeping the left heel flat on the court, bend the right knee while leaning the trunk forward (Figure 5.6b) to feel the stretch in the calf. Do not arch the lower back. To feel the stretch in the left heel, slightly bend the left knee and raise the left heel about 2 inches off the court. The left foot must be pointing forward throughout the exercise. Repeat the stretch for the right leg.

Figure 5.6 Fence stretch.

Arm Hang—Stand facing the fence with the knees slightly bent. Hold onto the fence with hands about shoulder width apart and let the body drop down, as shown in Figure 5.7.

Figure 5.7 Arm hang.

Racket Stretch—Hold the racket in the left hand, drape it over the left shoulder, and grasp it from behind the back with the right hand. Slowly pull down, stretching the left arm. Then pull up, stretching the right arm (see Figure 5.8). Switch arms and repeat the exercise.

Figure 5.8 Racket stretch.

Forearm Stretch—Stand holding the right arm in front of the body with the elbow completely straight and the palm down. Use the left hand to slowly stretch the wrist back, as shown in Figure 5.9a. Next, slowly stretch the right wrist down, as shown in Figure

5.9b. Turn the right palm up and repeat the first two stretches, then repeat the exercise for the left wrist.

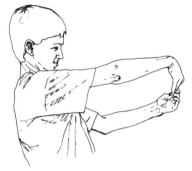

Figure 5.9   Forearm stretch.

Neck Semicircles—Standing with the head bent to the right (right ear toward the right shoulder), make a half-circle with the neck going forward (chin to chest), then bring the left ear toward the left shoulder. Next, bring the head to a neutral position and turn to look over the right shoulder as far as possible. Then turn to look over the left shoulder as far as possible.

As practice is winding down, slow players' heart rates with an easy jog or walk. Then arrange for a 5- to 10-minute period of easy stretching at the end of practice to help players avoid stiff muscles and make them less tight before the next practice.

What if One of My Players Gets Hurt?

No matter how good and thorough your prevention program, injuries will occur. When injury does strike, chances are you will be the one in charge. The severity and nature of the injury will determine how actively involved you'll be in treating the injury. But regardless of how seriously a player is hurt, it is your responsibility to know what steps to take. So let's look at how you can provide basic emergency care to your injured players.

Minor Injuries

Although no injury seems minor to the person experiencing it, most injuries are neither life-threatening nor severe enough to restrict participation. When such injuries occur, you can take an active role in their initial treatment.

Scrapes and Cuts

When one of your players has an open wound, follow these three steps.

1. *Stop the bleeding* by applying direct pressure with a clean dressing to the wound and elevating. Do not remove the dressing if it becomes blood-soaked. Instead, place an additional dressing on top of the one already in place. If bleeding continues, elevate the injured area above the heart and maintain pressure.

2. *Cleanse the wound* thoroughly once the bleeding is controlled. A good rinsing with a forceful stream of water, and perhaps light scrubbing with soap, will help prevent infection.

3. *Protect the wound* with sterile gauze or a Band-Aid. If the player continues to participate, apply protective padding over the injured area.

For bloody noses not associated with serious facial injury, have the athlete sit and lean slightly forward. Then pinch the player's nostrils shut. If the bleeding continues after several minutes or if the athlete has a history of nosebleeds, seek medical assistance.

Sprains and Strains

The physical demands of tennis practices and games often result in injury to the muscles or tendons (strains) or to the ligaments (sprains). When your players suffer minor strains or sprains, immediately apply the RICE method of injury care.

Bumps and Bruises

Occasionally a tennis player will fall on the court or collide with a doubles partner. If the force of a body part at impact is great enough, a bump or bruise will result. Many players continue playing with such sore spots, but if the bump or bruise is large and painful, you should act appropriately. Enact the RICE method of injury care and monitor the injury. If swelling, discoloration, and pain have lessened, the player may resume participation; if not, the player should be examined by a physician.

Serious Injuries

Head, neck, and back injuries; fractures; heat illness; and injuries that cause a player to lose consciousness are among a class of injuries that you cannot and should not try to treat yourself. But you should plan what you'll do if such an injury occurs. And your plan should include the following guidelines for action:

- Obtain the phone number and ensure the availability of nearby emergency care units.
- Assign an assistant coach or another adult the responsibility of contacting emergency medical help upon your request.
- Do not move the injured athlete.
- Calm the injured athlete, and keep others away from him or her as much as possible.
- Evaluate whether the athlete's breathing is stopped or irregular, and if necessary clear the airway with your fingers.
- Administer artificial respiration if breathing has stopped. Have a trained individual administer CPR if the athlete's circulation has stopped.
- Remain with the athlete until medical personnel arrive.

How Do I Protect Myself?

When one of your players is injured, naturally your first concern is his or her well-being. Your feelings for children, after all, are what made you decide to coach. Unfortunately,

---

The RICE Method

R—Rest the area to avoid further damage and foster healing.

I —Ice the area to reduce swelling and pain.

C—Compress the area by securing an ice bag in place with an elastic wrap.

E—Elevate the injury above heart level to keep the blood from pooling in the area.

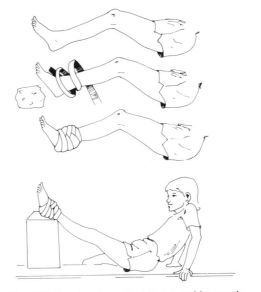

The RICE method applied to an ankle sprain.

there is something else that you must consider: Can you be held liable for the injury?

From a legal standpoint, a coach has nine duties to fulfill. We've discussed all but planning (see unit 4) in this unit.

1. Provide a safe environment.
2. Properly plan the activity.
3. Provide adequate and proper equipment.
4. Match or equate players.
5. Warn of inherent risks in tennis.
6. Supervise the activity closely.
7. Evaluate players for injury or incapacity.
8. Know emergency procedures and first aid.
9. Keep adequate records.

In addition to fulfilling these nine legal duties, you should check your insurance coverage to make sure your present policy will protect you from liability.

Summary Self-Test

Now that you've read how to make your coaching experience safe for your players

and yourself, test your knowledge of the material by answering these questions:

1. What are seven injury prevention measures you can institute to try to keep your players from getting hurt?
2. What is the three-step emergency care process for cuts?
3. What method of treatment is best for minor sprains and strains?
4. What steps can you take to manage serious injuries?
5. What are the nine legal duties of a coach?

UNIT 6

What Is Tennis All About?

From reading the first part of this manual you've gotten a good general understanding of what it takes to coach. Now it's time to develop your Comprehension of the rules of the game.

What Are the Rules?

Tennis is played worldwide in accordance with the official rules established by the International Tennis Federation (ITF). The USTA adheres to those rules plus The Code. The Code consists of the "unwritten" rules of tennis, which custom and tradition dictate that players follow in unofficiated matches. The rules and The Code apply to both *singles* and *doubles* play.

The Tennis Court

Before you teach players the rules of singles and doubles, make sure that they are familiar with all the lines of a tennis court. If you have any doubt about what each line represents, refer to Figure 6.1. Then instruct and quiz your players to ensure that they know what all the court markings mean.

Singles Play

One-on-one tennis is played on the singles court and requires each player to have a basic repertoire of skills to be successful. More basic than that, however, each player must understand the guidelines for participating in a singles match.

Serving

Tennis points begin with one player, called the *server*, hitting the ball from behind the baseline over the net into the receiver's service box. To see who serves first, players will spin a racket or toss a coin (see Figure 6.2). The player who wins the spin or toss may choose or make the opponent choose to *serve* first, receive first, or pick an end of the court on which to start the match.

Here are some instructions to give players about serving:

1. Before serving, be sure that the *receiver* is ready to play.

Figure 6.2 Spinning the racket for first service.

2. When serving the first point, you must stand behind the baseline between the center mark and the right singles sideline. Remember, you cannot step on or over the baseline until after you've hit the ball.
3. Your first serve must go over the net into the receiver's service court. If the first serve does not go into the correct court, it is called a *fault*. A second fault, or *double fault*, results in a point being awarded to the receiver.

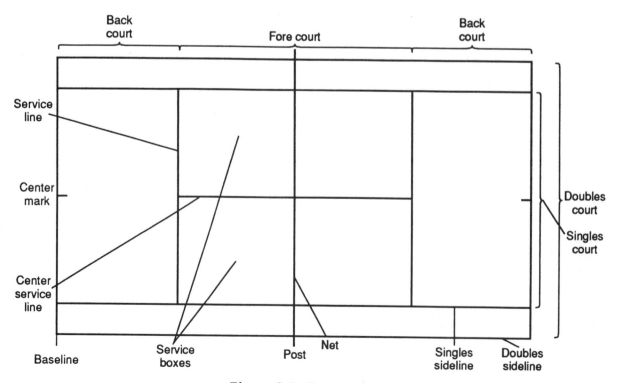

Figure 6.1 Tennis court.

4. If you serve a ball that hits the top of the net before bouncing into the correct service court, it's called a *let* (see Figure 6.3). The server serves again, with no penalty. If your serve hits the net and then goes outside the service court, it is ruled a fault.

Figure 6.3 Service let.

5. When serving the next point, you'll switch to a position behind the baseline between the center mark and the left sideline. You must then serve the ball into the receiver's left service court.

Have players switch ends of the court at the conclusion of the first game. The player who served the previous game will receive serve throughout the next game. Players should switch ends again after the third, fifth, and every following odd-numbered game.

Playing a Point

The serve is only the starting point in tennis. You must also teach players how to perform after the serve. Except when serving, a player may stand anywhere—in or out of the court—on her or his side of the net. Players also have the choice of hitting the ball before it bounces or after one bounce, but the receiver must let the serve bounce once before hitting it.

The ball is still in play if it happens to touch the net or post. And players should continue the point when a ball lands on a boundary line of the court.

A player wins the point if he or she hits the ball over the net into the court on the other side and the opponent does not return it. A player loses the point if she or he hits the ball into the net or out of the court (unless the opponent volleys the outgoing ball). A player also loses the point if the ball touches his or her clothing, if the racket touches the net or post, if the ball is hit before it passes the net, or if the ball is deliberately hit more than once. Players are on their honor to make these calls against themselves.

Scoring

When players are ready to begin playing games, they'll need to know how to score. Here is a point-by-point scoring protocol that you can teach your players. Before long, the scoring system will become second nature to them.

1. The first point won by a player is *15*; the player with no points has *Love*.
2. If the next point is won by the same player, the score is *30*-Love.
3. If that player then wins the 3rd and 4th points, the score is *40*-Love and finally *game*.
4. If any of the points is won by the opposing player, the scoring may be 15-Love, 15-all, 15-30, 30-all, 30-40, or game (with the opponent being the game winner).
5. If each player wins 3 points to tie the game at 40-40, the score is called *deuce*. The player who wins the next point has the *advantage*, often called *ad in* for the server and *ad out* for the receiver. If the player with the advantage wins the next point, she or he wins the game; if not, the score goes back to deuce. Then the first player to score 2 points in a row after deuce wins the game.
6. Players must call the score of the set (such as 4-3) before they serve for the first point of the game. They must also call the game score just before serving for each point, as in Figure 6.4. The server's score is always said first.

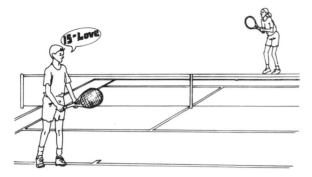

Figure 6.4 Calling out the score before serving.

7. The first player to win at least six games and to be ahead by at least two games wins a *set*. The first one to win two sets wins the *match*. If the score reaches six games all, players may play a *tie-break game* ("tie breaker"). Whoever wins this game wins the set.

12-Point Tie-Break Game. If announced in advance of the match, a tie-break game may be used when the score reaches six games all in any set. The player (or doubles team) who first wins 7 points wins the game and the set provided he or she leads by a margin of 2 points. If the score reaches 6 points all, the game is extended until this margin has been achieved. Numerical scoring (1, 2, 3, etc.) is used throughout the tie-break game.

The player whose turn it is to serve is the server for the first point; the opponent is the server for the 2nd and 3rd points; and, thereafter, each player serves alternately for 2 consecutive points until the winner of the game and set has been decided.

Starting with the first point, serves are delivered alternately from the right and left courts, beginning from the right. The first server serves the first point from the right court; the second server serves the 2nd and 3rd points from the left and right courts, respectively; and so on.

Players change ends after every 6 points and at the conclusion of the tie-break game. The player (or doubles team) who served first in the tie-break game should receive serve in the first game of the following set.

9-Point Tie-Break Game. The 9-point tie-break game is sometimes used in sets played under *no-ad* scoring. The player who first wins 5 points wins the game and set. Numerical scoring (1, 2, 3, etc.) is used throughout the tie-break game.

In singles, the player whose turn it is to serve is the server for the first and 2nd points, into the right service court and then the left service court; the opponent is the server for the 3rd and 4th points, right and left. Players change ends. The first server serves the 5th and 6th points, right and left; the opponent serves the 7th and 8th points, right and left. If the score reaches 4 points all, the second server serves the final point of the tie-break game into either the right or left court, whichever the opponent chooses.

In doubles, each player serves from the same end of the court that she or he served from during the set. The players stay on the same ends for one game of the next set, with the player (or doubles team) who served second in the tie-break game now serving first.

Calling Lines

Players share the responsibility for making loud, sure, and honest line calls. Unless the opponent asks for help, they may make calls only on their own side of the net. The following are guidelines you should set for your players to help them make proper line calls:

- If the ball touches any part of the line, it is good. Call the ball *out* only if you can clearly see a space between where the ball lands on the court and the line, as in Figure 6.5.
- Make any out call immediately.
- If you can't see whether a ball is definitely out, continue playing the point.
- A call can't be changed, even if a ball mark found after the point indicates a previous *shot* was out. The point stands as played.
- If you fail to see whether a ball that goes past you stays in or goes out, you must award the point to your opponent.
- A player loses the point for catching the ball on the fly, no matter where the player thinks it might land and even if the player is standing outside of the court.

Figure 6.5 Calling a ball out.

Doubles Play

Young tennis players enjoy playing one-on-one matches, but don't be surprised if many of your players prefer the game of doubles. In doubles, a player and a partner play against a pair of players on the other side of the net. To accommodate the extra players, the tennis court (see p. 36) is expanded to its full dimensions, from doubles sideline to doubles sideline. You must ensure that your players are aware of the following rules before they compete in doubles play.

- Either player on the team serving first may begin the match. Either person on the opposing team may receive the first ball in the right (or deuce) court.
- The receiving team may choose which player will play which court. They must then keep the same order of serving and the same sides for receiving for the whole set.
- If the server's partner is hit with the serve, a fault is called. If the receiver's partner is hit with the serve, the server wins the point.
- In returning shots (except the serve), either member of a doubles team may hit the ball. In other words, one partner may hit consecutive returns.

Court Conduct

It is imperative that you Comprehend the rules. However, the Communication and Character coaching tools are of equal importance in teaching players proper court behavior. You must both convey the importance of good conduct *and* exhibit it in your own actions if you expect your players to behave appropriately. Here is a checklist that you should encourage your players to follow:

- ☐ When standing near a tennis court in use, talk quietly so as not to disturb those who are playing (see Figure 6.6). Never walk behind a court in use until those playing have finished their point. This can be distracting to them.

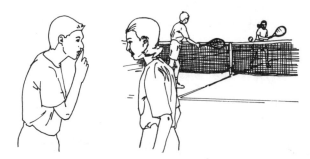

Figure 6.6 Keeping quiet while others play.

- ☐ When you're ready to play, put racket covers, ball cans, jackets, and the like, out of everyone's way.
- ☐ Introduce yourself to your opponent before warming up.
- ☐ Limit warm-up before a match to approximately 5 minutes. Hit balls back and forth with your opponent and take a few practice serves.
- ☐ In doubles, help your partner with line calls when possible. If your partner calls a ball out and you think it actually hit the line, you must call the ball good.
- ☐ Keep the game moving. Attempts to stall or to extend rest periods are illegal. Readily accept all calls made by your opponent.
- ☐ Intentional distractions that interfere with your opponent's concentration or

effort to play the ball are against the rules.

☐ If a serve is out, don't return it. Just tap it gently into the net or let it go behind you.

☐ If the ball goes into the next court, wait until the players on that court finish their point before asking for the ball. If a ball from an adjacent court comes onto yours, return it as soon as play has stopped on both courts.

☐ If there is any disagreement on the score, go back to the last score you and your opponent agree on, or spin a racket, with the winner setting the score.

☐ After the last point, come to the net quickly and shake hands with your opponent (see Figure 6.7). Let your opponents know you appreciated the match, no matter what the outcome.

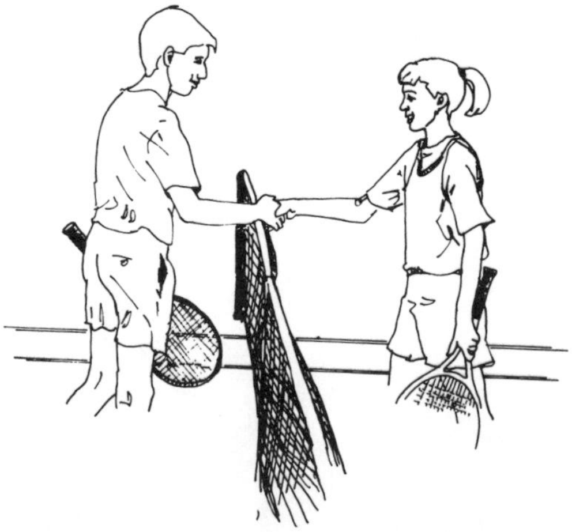

Figure 6.7 Postmatch handshake.

If players and their opponents cooperate in following the rules of tennis and treat each other with respect, they'll all get the most enjoyment from the game, whether they win or lose.

Summary Test

Now that you've read the basic tennis information in this unit, you should be able to answer a number of questions about the game. To test yourself, take the following quiz:

Tennis Court Matching Exercise (refer to Figure 6.8)

1. _____ Center service line

2. _____ Baseline

3. _____ Right service court

Scoring—True or False

4. _____ When the server wins the first point of the game, the score is love-15.

5. _____ The score is 40-40. The next point determines the game winner.

6. _____ The score is 4-2, a total of six games. The set is finished.

Rules and Etiquette—Multiple Choice

7. _____ How many chances does a player have to hit a good serve before losing the point?
   a. one   b. two   c. three

8. _____ On return of serve, the receiver must hit the ball
   a. after it bounces once   b. before it bounces
   c. either before or after it bounces once

9. _____ During a point, a ball that lands on the baseline is considered
   a. a let   b. a fault   c. a good ball

Answers: 1. c, 2. a, 3. d, 4. f, 5. f, 6. f, 7. b, 8. a, 9. c

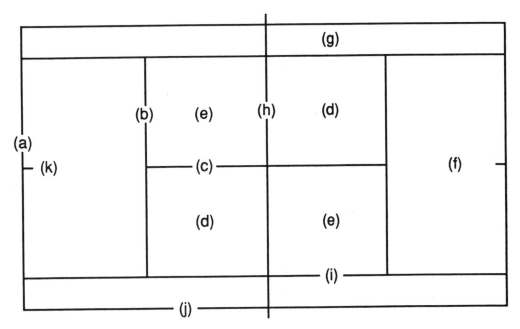

Figure 6.8 Tennis court matching exercise.

UNIT 7

What Tennis Skills and Drills Should I Teach?

Tennis is a sport that requires adept individual skills. And a player with little understanding of or training in these techniques has little chance of success. Therefore, it is important that you instruct your players well in these tennis skills and organize drills effectively so they can develop them. This unit tells you how.

Racket Control

The most basic skill in tennis is the *stroke* or swing. And the most important element of any tennis stroke is the contact point, the point at which the ball meets the racket face. Regardless of a player's stroke pattern or body position, the ball will go wherever the racket face is pointing at contact. The grip a player uses determines the racket face angle at the contact point, so your players must know and use the proper grip for each stroke.

Ball Control

Once players are able to grip the racket properly and begin stroking the ball, you'll need to teach them proper shot placement. Here are five key concepts that will help your players learn and improve their control of the tennis ball.

Height—Because tennis is a net game, the first challenge in any stroke is getting the ball over the net. The height of the tennis ball is controlled by "opening" or "closing" the racket face. An open racket face is one that is pointed toward the sky, as shown in Figure 7.1a. A closed racket face points at the ground, shown in Figure 7.1b. By contacting the ball with a slightly open racket face, the player will get the ball high enough to clear

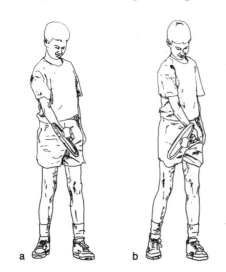

Figure 7.1 (a) Open racket face; (b) closed racket face.

the net. If a player is continually hitting the ball into the net, instruct the player to open the racket face slightly at the contact point.

Direction—Help players learn how to place the ball in different parts of the court to move the opponent around. Again, the angle of the racket face at contact controls the direction of the ball. Teach players how to contact the ball with the racket face pointed to the right (the ball will go right) and to the left (the ball will go left). Then they'll be able to keep their opponents on the move.

Depth—To keep an opponent from attacking (moving toward the net), a player's shots must land deep in the court. The easiest and most consistent way to get sufficient depth is to hit the ball higher over the net. Work with players so they can achieve sufficient depth without hitting every shot beyond the baseline.

Power—Shot placement is more effective if the ball gets to the spot quickly, making it difficult for the opponent to return. The speed at which a ball travels is determined by the size and speed of the swing used to stroke the ball; a very short, slow swing produces a weak return, and a very large, fast swing generates a great deal of pace. However, warn players that as they increase the power of their stroke, they decrease their ability to control the shot.

Spin—The use of *spin* lets players gain more control of their powerful shots. By imparting various types of spin, a player no longer must rely solely on gravity to keep shots in the court. It's essential that you teach players who wish to increase the accuracy of their more powerful shots how to use spins.

How Do I Use Tennis Drills Effectively?

The key to the effective use of tennis drills is to maintain control of each activity. Here are several tips for keeping drills under control:

- Make the purpose of each drill or activity clear.
- Give specific directions to players regard-

ing such things as where to line up, what task is to be performed, and which court area to hit into.

- Choose groups in a variety of ways— randomly, by best and worst at a particular skill, by overall ability, or by month of birth, just to name a few. Change groups frequently to maintain enthusiasm.
- Feeding of tennis balls should be "friendly," with minimal tossing and retrieving.
- Set up targets for players to hit to (racket covers, towels, frisbees).
- Use dead ball drills (after the player hits one ball fed by the coach, a second ball is fed) when introducing a skill.
- Advance to live ball drills (the ball is fed and kept in play) as players practice and improve.

Learning by Areas of the Court

The USTA National Coaches believe that the drills and activities you select should encourage players to master their performance in each area of the court. For example, the net play lessons teach more than how to *volley*— they tell you how to instruct players to play the net. So even if you're a first-time coach, you can help your players learn to perform consistent and winning volleys and *overheads*.

Here's the sequence to follow to develop your players' tennis skills for league play:

Baseline	1. Serve
	2. Forehand Ground-stroke
	3. Backhand Ground-stroke
	4. Lob
Midcourt	5. Forehand
	6. Backhand
	7. Transition Game
Net	8. Volley
	9. Overhead Smash
	10. Coverage
Doubles play	11. Serve & Volley
Specialty shots	12. Spins

Practice
#1

What Tennis Drills Should I Use?

The drills and activities in this section are designed for the average *Junior Team Tennis* player who has played enough tennis to maintain brief rallies from baseline to baseline. For additional drills and activities for varying ability levels, contact the USTA.

Practice #1

Baseline: The Serve

Performance Objective. Players will be able to hit full-swing baseline serves using the proper grip.

Introduce the Serve

Bring players into a semicircle around you.

1. Introduce yourself.
2. Summarize the objectives for the season: to have fun, to increase consistency of all shots, to begin to feel comfortable playing in all areas of the court, and to develop new specialty shots like the spin serve.

3. Review key rules:

- No hitting balls or swinging rackets until you give the word.
- No talking when the team is called together.
- When you address the team, everyone is to hold the racket against the chest with crossed arms (demonstrate).

4. "For our first practice we are going to learn how to hit full-swing serves. The serve is the most important stroke in the game of tennis because it is used to start every point."

Practice
#1

Figure 7.2　The serve.

Demonstrate the Serve

From the service line, demonstrate three or four full-swing serves (see Figures 7.2a-f) from various angles before your players. Show them how the serve resembles an overhand throw.

Explain the Serve

Point out the elements of continental grip (see Figure 7.3), stance, backswing and toss, contact point, and follow-through.

Attend to Players Practicing

Warm-Up Activity: Groundstroke & Dig *(4 minutes).*
Have players form a single-file line behind the

Figure 7.3　The continental grip.

baseline. One at a time, feed each player a forehand groundstroke and a drop-shot to the backhand. Players jog to pick up balls they've just hit and return to the end of the line (see Figure 7.4).

Stretching *(6 minutes).* Bring players into a circle around you to perform the stretches in unit 5 (pages 30-32). While all are stretching, ask players to introduce themselves in turn and to summarize their tennis background.

Serve Drills

Serve Assessment *(5 minutes).* With players spread out along the baseline, observe their technique during warm-up serves. Players having difficulty performing a proper full-swing serve should be taken through the Serve Progression. Those already comfortable with a full-swing serve should move to a separate court and complete the Parallel Activity.

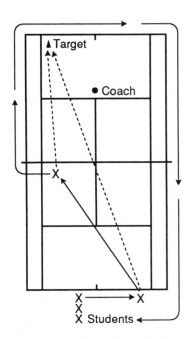

Figure 7.4 Groundstroke and dig activity.

Safety Tip

Whenever players are lined up to hit full-swing serves, they must follow your commands on when to serve and when to pick up. This will prevent a player who is retrieving a ball being hit by a server. Keep all other players well behind the servers until you tell servers to pick up their balls.

Serve Progression *(12 minutes).* Position players in up to four lines perpendicular to the net. Have players observe your demonstration. Then have them model the following progression:

1. **Stance**—Sideways to net.
2. **Grip**—Hold racket up on edge toward net with nondominant hand and grip like a hammer with the racket hand.
3. **Backswing**—Drop both arms together and raise the racket arm to shoulder height with the knuckles pointed up and the racket pointed to the back fence.
4. **Backswing, Bend, and Extend**—Take a backswing, bend the racket arm at the elbow, then extend upward with the racket hand facing the net (repeat).
5. **Backswing, Bend, Extend, and Shift**—Repeat the extension and add weight transfer from the back to the front foot by opening the hips toward the net and leaving only the toe of the back foot touching the ground.
6. **Backswing, Toss, and Tap**—Standing near the fence, take a backswing, toss a ball, and bend and extend the racket, tapping the ball against the fence. Check for proper grip and full extension (repeat).
7. **Backswing, Toss, Tap, and Follow-Through**—Have players form four lines behind the service line. The first player in each line stands 4 feet from the net and "tap-serves" four balls over the net, following through slowly across the body to the opposite hip. The player retrieves the four balls and returns to the end of the line.
8. **Full Swing**—Players slowly perform toss and full backswing together, tap, and follow through.

Parallel Activity: Target Serve. Position players in two single-file lines per court, behind the baseline. Each player serves four balls to a target placed in each service box, then goes to the end of the other line. When all balls have been hit, players pick them up and begin serving again. (If players request or need additional incentives, they can keep score, with 1 point for every successful serve and 3 points for hitting the target.)

Error Detection and Correction for the Serve

ERROR	CORRECTION
1. Using an improper grip	1. Start with the continental and squeeze the grip when the racket passes behind the head
2. Leading with the elbow	2a. Use the proper grip b. Reach up to contact, then serve and freeze at contact
3. Hitch in the swing	3a. Coach guides the player's arm through in slow motion b. Perform two complete motions, one after the other, the first with no toss and the second with a toss and hit

Serve Practice—Height Control *(5 minutes)*. Have each player place four balls on the court: 4 feet from the net, on the service line, at ¾ court, and on the baseline. On command, players serve the balls over the net, progressing from the net to the baseline. Once all balls have been hit, players retrieve and repeat. Stress the use of the proper serve grip.

Coaching Tip

Successful servers get a high percentage of serves in the court. So remind your players that a few dazzling aces among several double faults are not nearly as effective as hitting serves that always go in and therefore must always be returned.

Serve & Return—Directional Control *(6 minutes)*. Form two lines of servers on one side of each court and two lines of receivers on the opposite side. Each server hits two balls to the correct service box and goes to the end of the serving line. Each receiver returns the two serves cross-court and goes to the end of the receiving line. Have teams switch roles so players can work on the opposite stroke.

Team Singles *(10 minutes)*. Have equal groups line up single-file behind the baseline and on opposite sides of the net. One at a time, each player plays one point of a singles game, then returns to the end of the line. Play as many games as time permits. If ample courts are available, have players play regular singles.

Ball Reaction Drill *(5 minutes)*. Position players in up to four lines parallel to and facing the net. Facing players from the opposite side of the net, hold up one tennis ball. Instruct players that they are to shuffle from side to side, forward and back as you move the ball in those directions. Players shuffle for 20 seconds, rest for 20 seconds. Take players through the drill four times.

Sportsmanship Tip
Models of Etiquette (5 minutes)

Have two players play a mock singles game in front of the team to review scoring for both games and sets. Emphasize proper court etiquette.

Practice Evaluation and Cool-Down *(5 minutes)*. With players in a semicircle facing you, have them perform some light stretches to cool down. Briefly review and evaluate the day's activities. Ask players to practice their serves 15 minutes each to the *deuce court* and ad court, with or without a partner, before the next practice session.

Practice #2

Baseline:
The Forehand Groundstroke

Performance Objectives. Players will develop correct technique for the forehand *groundstroke* using the proper grip and will continue to improve the serve.

Review the Serve. Briefly review the serving elements of continental grip, stance, backswing and toss, contact point, and follow-through. Ask who practiced their serves since the last session.

Introduce the Forehand Groundstroke

"Today we will warm up, stretch, and then work on the forehand groundstroke." Tell your players that the forehand groundstroke is used to strike a ball on the racket side of the body after it has bounced.

Demonstrate the Forehand Groundstroke

From the service line and with players standing in the *alley*, demonstrate a forehand drive (see Figure 7.5a-e) by using a drop-hit (dropping the ball to your racket side and stroking it over the net). Next, demonstrate the forehand return of serve with only a shoulder turn, contact, and follow-through.

Explain the Forehand Groundstroke

Point out the elements of the eastern "shake hands" grip (see Figure 7.6), ready position, shoulder turn, racket back and down, adjusting steps, contact point, and follow-through.

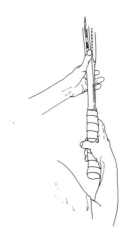

Figure 7.6 Forehand grip.

Attend to Players Practicing

Warm-Up Activity: Groundstroke & Dig *(4 minutes)*. See page 46.

Stretching *(6 minutes)*. See pages 30-32.

Forehand Drills

Forehand Practice *(8 minutes)*. Two groundstrokers stand on the service line of the deuce and ad courts. Two feeders face them from the same position on the opposite side of the net. Two retrievers line up behind the feeders at the baseline. The feeder tosses the ball to the forehand side of the groundstroker, who hits a forehand down the line while concentrating on finishing with a long, high follow-through. Each groundstroker hits five balls and then moves to retrieving position. The retriever moves to the feeding position and the feeder becomes a

Figure 7.5 Forehand groundstroke.

groundstroker. Have groundstrokers progress from service line to ¾ court to baseline after each complete rotation.

Forehand Rallies *(12 minutes).*   Players work six to a court. With partners across the net from each other in the doubles alleys and in the center of the court, have players complete the following forehand consistency progression:

1. In midcourt rallies, players work to hit 10 forehand groundstrokes in a row without an error.
2. Once a pair hits the ball 10 times in a row, they can back up to ¾ court.
3. If they hit 10 forehands in a row from ¾ court, both players move to the baseline and engage in full-court rallies. All shots must land beyond the service line. Challenge pairs to hit a record number of deep shots.

Safety Tip

When positioned for drills, players must remain in their designated areas even if their balls leave their areas.

Forehand Return of Serve *(5 minutes).*   Two hitters stand in returning position in the deuce and ad courts. Two servers stand on the opposite service line, with two retrievers behind them on the baseline, as shown in Figure 7.7. The server feeds the ball into the proper service box for the hitter to return cross-court. Retrievers pick up balls. Hitters return five forehands, then move to retrieving position. Retrievers serve the balls they have picked up and the servers become returners.

Rotating Team Rallies *(5 minutes).*   With teams lined up single-file behind each baseline, put the ball into play with a drop-hit from outside the

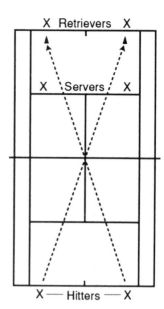

Figure 7.7   Forehand Return of Serve drill.

doubles alley near the service line. The first player in line hits a cross-court forehand and quickly returns to the end of the line so the next teammate may continue the rally. Teams score points for every ball hit successfully cross-court.

Serve & Forehand Rallies *(5 minutes).*   From the same formation used in the Forehand Return of Serve drill but with servers behind the baseline, players serve, return, and rally forehands cross-court for a record number of hits.

Conditioning—Toss & Catch *(5 minutes).*   Divide team into pairs of tossers and catchers standing 6 feet apart and facing each other. Pairs should be positioned throughout the entire court area so they have plenty of space to move about. Holding two balls, the tosser tosses one ball between 1 and 6 feet in any direction. The catcher must quickly move to catch the ball after its first bounce and toss it back to the tosser. As soon as the catcher catches one ball, the tosser quickly

---

Error Detection and Correction for the Forehand

ERROR	CORRECTION
1. Mistiming or overhitting shots	1. Shorten the backswing
2. Lack of height or directional control	2a. Check for proper grip
	b. Stop at contact to check the racket face
	c. Follow-through high and toward the target

tosses the second ball in another direction. Catchers catch for 20 seconds, then become tossers for 20 seconds. Take players through this rotation four times.

Practice Evaluation and Cool-Down *(5 minutes)*. Review and evaluate the practice while players perform light stretches. Ask each player to set a record for continuous forehand rallies with a partner before the next practice. All balls must land in the singles court and must be returned on one bounce.

Sportsmanship Tip
Calling Lines (5 minutes)

Have players stand on one baseline. On the opposite side of the court place seven balls on and near the baseline. Ask players to make an "in" or "out" call on each ball using the proper hand signal. Indicate whether the ball was in or out after they make the call. Then have them walk around and see whether they were correct. They will better appreciate the difficulty in making calls from the opposite side of the net, even when a ball is stationary. Point out that because it is so hard to determine exactly where a ball lands from the other side of the net, they should not question opponents' calls.

Practice #3

Baseline:
The Backhand Groundstroke

Performance Objective. Players will develop correct technique for the backhand groundstroke using the proper grip.

Review the Forehand. Review the grip, ready position, shoulder turn, backswing, adjusting steps, contact, and follow-through on the forehand groundstroke.

Introduce the Backhand

"Today we will warm up, stretch, and then work on the backhand groundstroke. The backhand groundstroke is used to strike a ball on the nonracket side of the body after it has bounced."

Demonstrate the Backhand

With players standing in the doubles alley, show the one- and two-handed eastern backhand grips shown in Figures 7.8a and 7.8b. Check all grips; then, from the service line, demonstrate a drop-hit one-handed (see Figures 7.9a-d) and two-handed (see Figure 7.10a-d) backhand groundstroke.

Explain the Backhand

Explain the ready position, grip change as the racket is taken back with the thumb touching the opposite pocket, adjusting steps, contact, and

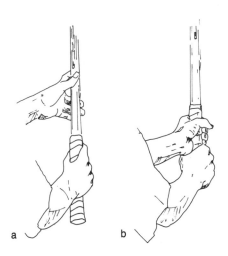

Figure 7.8 Backhand grips: (a) one-handed, (b) two-handed.

long follow-through. Players may use one- or two-handed backhands, but require all to make the proper grip change.

Attend to Players Practicing

Warm-Up Activity: Forehand Rallies *(4 minutes)*. See page 50.

Stretching *(6 minutes)*. See pages 30-32.

Backhand Drills

Backhand Practice *(8 minutes)*. Two groundstrokers stand on the service line of the deuce and ad courts. Two feeders face them from the same

Figure 7.9 One-handed backhand groundstroke.

Figure 7.10 Two-handed backhand groundstroke.

position on the opposite side of the net (same as Forehand Practice on page 49). Two retrievers line up behind the feeders at the baseline. The feeder tosses the ball to the backhand side of the groundstroker, who hits backhands down the line. Each groundstroker should hit five balls and then move to retrieving position. The retriever moves to the feeding position and the feeder becomes a groundstroker. Have groundstrokers progress from service line to ¾ court to baseline after each complete rotation. Stress a long, high follow-through on the stroke for proper ball height over the net.

Coaching Tip

Most players find successful backhand shots harder to make than forehands. However, most experienced coaches find it easier to teach the backhand than the forehand, perhaps because there's much less variance in form among successful backhands. Using a two-handed backhand tends to bring players quicker success, and should be encouraged for those players finding major frustrations. If proper technique (grip and stroke patterns) are taught, players can rapidly improve their backhand strokes.

Error Detection and Correction for the Backhand

ERROR	CORRECTION
1. Leads with elbow	1. Place the thumb of the dominant hand on the opposite hip and "throw" the racket like a frisbee
2. Lack of height or directional control	2a. Check the grip b. Stop at contact to check the racket face c. Extend the follow-through high and toward the target

Backhand Rallies *(12 minutes)*. Players work six to a court. With partners across the net from each other in each doubles alley and in the center of the court (as in Forehand Rallies on page 50), have players complete the following backhand consistency progression (when forehands are hit they do not have to start over but may not count the stroke in their scores):

1. Have players begin with midcourt backhand rallies. Encourage players to hit 10 backhand groundstrokes in a row without an error.
2. Once a pair hits the ball 10 times in a row, they can back up to ¾ court.
3. If they hit 10 backhands in a row from ¾ court, both players can move to the baseline and engage in full-court rallies. All shots must land beyond the service line. Challenge pairs to hit a record number of deep shots.

Backhand Return of Serve *(5 minutes)*. Two hitters stand in returning position in the deuce and ad courts. Two servers stand on the opposite service line, with two retrievers behind them on the baseline (same as Forehand Return of Serve on page 50). The server feeds the ball into the proper service box for the hitter to return crosscourt. Retrievers pick up balls. Hitters return five backhands, then move to retrieving position. Retrievers serve the balls they have picked up and the servers become returners.

Team Baseline Game *(5 minutes)*. Divide the group into two teams, which stand well behind the baseline on opposite sides of the net. Two groundstrokers from each team stand on the baseline with teammates behind. Put the ball into play with a drop-hit from outside the doubles alley near the service line. Players play out the point two against two. When the point is completed, two new players from each team move up to the baseline to play the next point. Team scores are kept, with players rotating after every point.

Sportsmanship Tip
Role-Playing to Teach (5 minutes)

An effective way to make a point about proper court conduct is to role-play the following two types of players. The first is a courteous, cooperative opponent who hits the ball under control in the warm-up and asks such questions as "Would you like to try some volleys?" The second is a player who is determined to smash every ball for a winner and complains every time the opponent doesn't get the ball back over the net. Ask your players which opponent they would prefer and why.

Conditioning—Roll & Catch *(5 minutes)*. Same as Toss & Catch on page 50, except the tosser rolls the ball on the ground. Take players through four rotations of rolling for 20 seconds and catching for 20 seconds.

Practice Evaluation and Cool-Down *(5 minutes)*. Review and evaluate the practice while players perform light stretches. Ask each player to set a record for continuous backhand rallies with a partner before the next practice. All balls must land in the singles court and must be returned on one bounce.

Practice #4

Baseline: The Lob

Performance Objectives.   Players will be able to execute the lob and will continue to improve groundstroke consistency.

Review the Backhand.   Briefly review the grip, ready position, shoulder turn, backswing, adjusting steps, contact, and follow-through on the backhand groundstroke.

Introduce the Lob

"Today we're going to continue to work on groundstroke consistency and learn how to hit the lob." Explain that lobs are used by a player who is out of position or when an opponent is at the net.

Demonstrate the Lob

From the baseline, demonstrate both the forehand and backhand lob from a drop-hit.

Explain the Lob

Point out how the preparation for a lob is identical to a groundstroke but that the racket face is slightly open and the follow-through is higher for greater loft.

Attend to Players Practicing

Warm-Up Activity: Backhand Rallies *(4 minutes).* See page 53.

Stretching *(6 minutes).*   See pages 30-32.

Lob Drills

Clear the Coach *(5 minutes).* Players line up single-file behind the ad court doubles alley. Feed one ball wide to the opposite corner; the first player runs the ball down and lobs over your head to a cross-court target. The player then quickly retrieves the ball just hit and returns to the end of the line (see Figure 7.11). Each player performs the drill five times. Move the line to the deuce court alley so players can work on the opposite stroke.

Coaching Tip

Place targets (racket covers, frisbees, or even towels) on the court for players to aim at during drills.

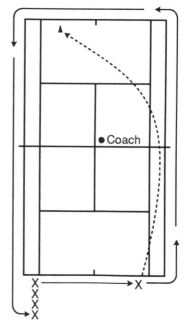

Figure 7.11   Clear-the-Coach drill.

Change of Direction *(5 minutes).*   Players line up single-file behind the ad court doubles alley. Feed three balls to the first player in line—down the middle of the court for a cross-court groundstroke, near the ad court sideline for a down-the-line groundstroke, and near the deuce court sideline for a lob. The player picks up the three balls just hit and returns to the end of the line. Each player performs the drill five times. Move the line to the deuce court alley so players can work on the opposite strokes.

Safety Tip

When two players are on the court and others are waiting to step on, the observers must be careful to wait well in back of the baseline (so as not to interfere with play or get hit with a backswing) and watch the action until it is their turn. Designate a safe waiting area for the on-deck team or player to keep players from crowding forward.

Alternate In *(10 minutes).*   Place two players on each baseline and alternates standing between but well behind them (see Figure 7.12). Have players rally lobs cross-court. When a player makes en error, he or she is replaced by an alternate.

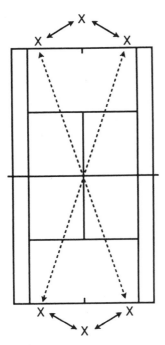

Figure 7.12 Alternate In drill.

Alternate In With Serve *(5 minutes).* Same as the Alternate In drill, but players start the rally with a Serve & Return.

Team Singles *(12 minutes).* See page 48.

Sportsmanship Tip
Spinning the Racket (2 minutes)

Show players how to spin the racket to determine who will serve first in a match. Discuss the options of serving or receiving and choosing a side of the court or making your opponent choose.

Conditioning—Toss, Roll, and Catch *(5 minutes).* Tosser randomly alternates tosses and rolls. Have players toss for 20 seconds, then catch for 20 seconds. Take players through this rotation four times.

Practice Evaluation and Cool-Down *(5 minutes).* Review and evaluate the practice while players perform light stretches. Ask each player to hit 20 cross-court drop-hit lobs from both the forehand and backhand sides before the next practice.

Error Detection and Correction for the Lob

ERROR	CORRECTION
No follow-through on the swing	Finish the stroke with the racket "high in the sky."

Practice #5

Midcourt: The Forehand

Performance Objective. Players will be able to move from the baseline to the net area on the forehand side.

Review the Lob. Briefly review that a lob should be disguised by using the same preparation as a groundstroke and that it is used by a player who is out of position or when an opponent is at the net.

Introduce the Midcourt Forehand

"Today we're going to learn how to play offensively on the forehand side by attacking short, weak returns and weak second serves."

Demonstrate the Midcourt Forehand

From the service line, demonstrate the three forehand shots that may be used in the midcourt area: a winner cross-court, an approach shot down the line, or a cross-court drop shot.

Explain the Midcourt Forehand

Point out that a winner is a difficult shot to hit consistently, an approach shot is a high-percentage shot, and a drop shot should only be used as a surprise. Explain that all these shots require that the player move through the shot using a shortened backswing. Players should aim for targets that risk only one line (few strategic shots demand hitting a ball close to two lines).

Coaching Tip

Don't limit your instruction to groundstrokes from the baseline and volleys at the net; teach your players how to handle balls landing in the midcourt area. If your players feel comfortable with their midcourt skills, they will be better able to attack the net.

Attend to Players Practicing

Warm-Up Activity: Forehand Rallies *(4 minutes).* See page 50.

Stretching *(6 minutes).* See pages 30-32.

Midcourt Forehand Drills

Forehand Winner *(4 minutes).* Players form a single-file line behind the baseline. Feed a short, high forehand inside the service line, the first player in line hits to a cross-court target placed near the sideline and just beyond the service line.

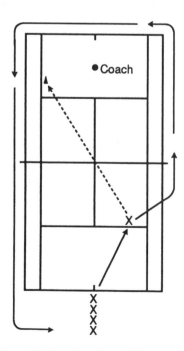

Figure 7.13 Forehand Winner drill.

The first player then retrieves the ball and returns to the end of the line (see Figure 7.13).

Forehand Approach *(8 minutes).* From the same formation used in the Forehand Winner drill but with a low bouncing feed, have players hit a controlled forehand down-the-line approach shot to a target placed near the baseline and several feet from the sideline. After a few rounds, feed a second ball to the players immediately after they hit the first approach shot. Have players hit a cross-court forehand (angle) volley to the corner of the service box on their second shots, as shown in Figure 7.14.

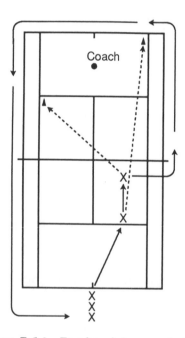

Figure 7.14 Forehand Approach drill.

Drop Shot *(4 minutes).* Using the same formation as the Forehand Winner and Approach drills and a medium height feed, have players hit a cross-court forehand drop shot that lands in the service box. Ask players to try to make the ball bounce three times before it leaves the service box.

Safety Tip

When overhead smashes are hit as part of an activity, feed all balls from the bucket first and have players pick up balls together. This will prevent players from being hit when retrieving balls.

Approach, Volley, Overhead *(5 minutes).* Position players as in the Forehand Winner and Approach drills. Feed each player a forehand approach, forehand volley, and an overhead. The player

---

Error Detection and Correction for the Midcourt Forehand

ERROR	CORRECTION
Overhitting midcourt shots	Shorten the backswing by simply placing the racket face behind the ball and following through

then returns to the end of the line. Have everyone pick up balls when the bucket is empty.

Transition Workup (12 minutes). The object of this game is to work up to the feeder's side of the court and stay there as long as possible. The formation starts with two players on the baseline defending the singles court. Remaining players line up single-file behind the opposite baseline. One of the baseline pair starts the point by feeding a short ball to the first player on the far side. The first player on the far side comes in and hits (based on the height of the bounce) an aggressive cross-court forehand, a down-the-line approach, or a drop shot and plays out the point one against two. If the approaching player wins, he or she sprints around the net (to the right) and takes the spot of the nearest baseliner, who moves to her or his right. The baseliner who had been playing the right side runs to the back of the approaching line and starts over. If the approaching player loses the point, he or she goes to the end of the hitting line.

Sportsmanship Tip
Fault and Let Serves (2 minutes)

Briefly explain that a serve that touches the net and lands in the proper service box is called a let *and must be replayed. If a serve goes into the net or does not land in the proper service box, a* fault *is called. Servers get two opportunities to serve into the correct service box on every point.*

Conditioning—Toss, Roll, Catch, and Check (5 minutes). This drill is the same as the Toss, Roll, and Catch drill on page 55. However, the tosser occasionally yells "Check," signaling the catcher to run up to and around the tosser and back to a position 6 feet away. Catchers catch for 20 seconds, then become tossers for 20 seconds. Take players through this rotation four times.

Practice Evaluation and Cool-Down (5 minutes). Review and evaluate the practice while players perform light stretches. Ask each player to play 10 consecutive points against a partner's midcourt forehand feed before the next practice.

Practice #6

Midcourt: Backhand

Performance Objective. Players will be able to move from the baseline to the net area on the backhand side.

Review the Midcourt Forehand. Remind players of the forehand winner, approach shot, and drop shot options from the midcourt area.

Introduce the Midcourt Backhand

"Now that you know how to play aggressively from the forehand side, we're going to practice the same shots from the backhand side."

Demonstrate the Midcourt Backhand

From the service line, demonstrate the winner, approach shot, and drop shot using both one- and two-handed backhands (see page 51).

Explain the Midcourt Backhand

As with the midcourt forehand, emphasize using a shortened backswing, moving through the ball, and aiming for targets.

Attend to Players Practicing

Warm-Up Activity: Backhand Rallies (4 minutes). See page 53.

Stretching (6 minutes). See pages 30-32.

Midcourt Backhand Drills

Backhand Winner *(6 minutes)*. Players form a single-file line behind the baseline (see Forehand Winner, page 56). Feed one short, high backhand inside the service line, which the first player in line hits to a cross-court target placed near the sideline and just beyond the service line. The first player then retrieves the ball and returns to the end of the line.

Coaching Tip

Players will often attempt to use the same long backswing in the midcourt area that they use from the baseline. Remind players that the closer they get to the net, the shorter the backswing must be.

Backhand Approach *(8 minutes)*. From the same formation used in the Backhand Winner drill but with a low bouncing feed, have players hit a controlled backhand down-the-line approach shot to a target placed near the baseline and several feet from the sideline. After a few rounds, feed a second ball, which players hit as a cross-court backhand (angle) volley to the corner of the service box.

Drop Shot *(4 minutes)*. Using the same formation as the Backhand Winner and Backhand Approach drills and a medium height feed, have players hit a cross-court backhand drop shot that lands in the service box. Ask players to try to make the ball bounce three times before it leaves the service box.

Approach, Volley, Overhead *(5 minutes)*. From the same formation as the Drop Shot drill, feed each player a backhand approach, backhand volley, and an overhead; then the player returns to the end of the line. Have everyone pick up balls when the bucket is empty and continue the drill.

Transition Workup *(12 minutes)*. See page 57. Players hit either forehand or backhand midcourt shots.

Sportsmanship Tip
Calling Out the Score (2 minutes)

Explain to players that as a courtesy and to avoid scoring problems during a match, the server calls out the score before every point.

Conditioning—React & Spring *(5 minutes)*. Divide the team into pairs of tossers and catchers, standing 6 feet apart and positioned throughout the entire court area. Have catchers stand with their backs to the tossers. Instruct tossers to toss or roll the ball in any direction and call "Go!" Upon hearing the signal, catchers must turn, recover the ball, and turn away to listen for the next cue. Catchers catch for 20 seconds, then become tossers for 20 seconds. Take players through this rotation four times.

Practice Evaluation and Cool-Down *(5 minutes)*. Review and evaluate the practice while players perform light stretches. Ask each player to play 10 consecutive points against a partner's midcourt backhand feed before the next practice.

Error Detection and Correction for the Midcourt Backhand

ERROR	CORRECTION
Opening shoulders and hips during the stroke	Stay sideways and use a carioca step (back foot crosses behind front foot) through the stroke

Practice #7

Midcourt: The Transition Game

Performance Objectives. Players will be able to hit a winner, an approach, and a drop shot from midcourt.

Review the Midcourt Backhand. Remind players of the backhand winner, approach shot, and drop shot options from the midcourt area.

Introduce the Transition Game

"After a brief warm-up and stretch, we're going to continue to work on approaching the net when our opponent hits a short, weak return or second serve."

Demonstrate the Transition Game

From the service line, demonstrate the winner, approach shot, and drop shot from both the forehand and backhand (one- and two-handed) sides.

Explain the Transition Game

Remind players that a winner is a difficult shot to hit consistently, an approach shot is a high-percentage shot, and a drop shot should be used only as a surprise. Emphasize using a shortened backswing, moving through the ball, and aiming for targets.

Attend to Players Practicing

Warm-Up Activity: Alternate In (4 minutes). See page 54.

Stretching (6 minutes). See pages 30-32.

Transition Drills

Winner (4 minutes). Players form a single-file line behind the baseline (as in Forehand Winner on page 56). Feed a short, high forehand or backhand inside the service line, which the first player in line hits to a cross-court target placed near the sideline and just beyond the service line. The first player then retrieves the ball and returns to the end of the line.

Approach & Volley (5 minutes). From the same formation used in the Winner drill but with a low bouncing feed, have players hit a controlled forehand or backhand approach shot down the line to a target placed near the baseline and several feet from the sideline. Feed a second ball that the players angle-volley cross-court to the corner of the service box. After three rounds, have players first hit a cross-court groundstroke, then an approach, and finally a volley.

Groundstroke and Drop Shot (5 minutes). Using the same formation as the Winner and the Approach & Volley drills and a medium height feed, have players hit a cross-court groundstroke and a cross-court drop shot from either the forehand or backhand side.

Half-Court Approach (10 minutes). On one half of the court players form two single-file lines behind opposite baselines. The first players from each line begin a rally with a drop-hit. Players rally, using only half the court, until one player makes an error or gets a short ball. The player receiving the short ball must hit an approach shot and play out the half-court point. Upon completion of the point, players return to the ends of their lines. Divide the team into four single-file lines and have two half-court points played at the same time.

> ### Coaching Tip
>
> *One of the big advances for a tennis player comes when a soft, short ball is transformed from a difficult get or an outright winner into an offensive opportunity. This has more to do with preparation, anticipation, and practice than raw speed.*

Team Singles (10 minutes). Refer to page 48. Encourage players to attack at every opportunity.

Conditioning—Line Sprints (5 minutes). Using one doubles sideline as the starting line, have players sprint to and touch the first singles sideline, return to touch the starting line, sprint and touch the center service line, return, sprint and

---

Error Detection and Correction for the Midcourt Shots

ERROR	CORRECTION
Stopping before hitting the shot	Push off of the back foot and run through the stroke

---

touch the far singles sideline, return, sprint and touch the far doubles sideline, and return to the starting line. Players sprint for 20 seconds, then rest for 20 seconds. Take players through this rotation four times.

Practice Evaluation and Cool-Down *(5 minutes)*. Review and evaluate the practice while players perform light stretches. Ask players to play 10 consecutive points against a partner's midcourt feed before the next practice.

> **Sportsmanship Tip**
> Continuous Play (2 minutes)
>
> *Explain to your players that play in tennis must be continuous. This means players must warm up all their strokes, including serves, during the warm-up period and that they may take no longer than 30 seconds between points once play has begun.*

Practice #8

Net Play: The Volley

Performance Objective.   Players will be able to execute the forehand and backhand volley.

Review the Transition Game.   Remind players to approach the net when their opponent hits a short, weak return or second serve by using the winner, approach shot, or drop shot.

Introduce the Volley

"During today's practice we're going to learn how to hit the volley." Point out that the volley is used when one is positioned at the net to hit the ball before it bounces. A player who can reach the net position during a point has a tremendous advantage. The net player has many more court angles to hit into, and the baseline opponent is forced to hit a difficult passing shot.

Demonstrate the Volley

Briefly demonstrate the ready position and crossover step as you block the ball on both the forehand and backhand volleys, shown in Figures 7.15 and 7.16, respectively.

Explain the Volley

Explain that the eastern forehand and backhand grips may be used for volleys but that little or no backswing is required for the stroke. Advanced players use a continental grip for both forehand and backhand volleys.

Attend to Players Practicing

Warm-Up Activity: Groundstroke Rallies *(4 minutes)*. Players may hit forehands or backhands (see pages 50 and 53).

Stretching *(6 minutes)*.   See pages 30-32.

Volley Drills

Volley Practice *(8 minutes)*.   Two volleyers stand in the service boxes of the deuce and ad courts. Two feeders face them from the same positions on the opposite side of the net. Two retrievers line up behind the feeders at the baseline. Feeders toss the ball alternately to the forehand and backhand sides of the volleyers, who hit volleys down the line. Each volleyer hits five balls and then moves to the retrieving position. The retriever moves to the feeding position and the feeder becomes a volleyer.

Figure 7.15   Forehand volley.

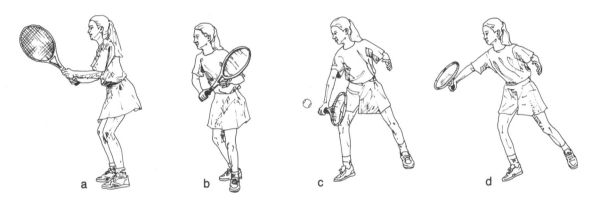

Figure 7.16   Backhand volley.

Error Detection and Correction for the Volley

ERROR	CORRECTION
1. Contact is made behind the body on the forehand	1. Cross the free arm over the hitting wrist
2. Jabbing the volley on the backhand	2a. Keep the elbow fairly straight and make certain the thumb is wrapped around the grip b. Cradle the racket with the free hand
3. Using the same racket face on both the forehand and backhand sides in a ''windshield wiper'' fashion	3. Place a piece of tape on the edge of the racket and make certain the tape always faces up

Coaching Tip

As in the midcourt area, a common mistake made by players when volleying is to take too big of a swing. Use key words or phrases like "block," "catch," and "squeeze and freeze" to remind players that the volley requires little or no racket movement.

***Two Volley** (5 minutes).* Players form a single-file line in the ad court doubles alley behind the service line, as shown in Figure 7.17. Feed two volleys to the first player in line, the first near the center service line and the second near the far sideline. The player hits the first ball to a target near the far sideline and angles the second ball to a target in the corner of the service box. The player moves diagonally toward the far net post to "cut off" both volleys, retrieves both balls, and returns to the end of the line. Each player performs the drill five times. Move the line to the deuce court doubles alley so players can work on the opposite stroke.

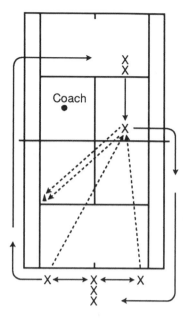

Figure 7.18 Groundstroke to Volley drill.

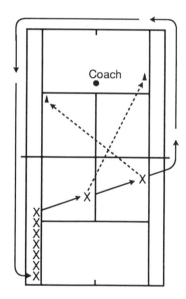

Figure 7.17 Two Volley drill.

***Groundstroke to Volley** (10 minutes).* Divide the team into single-file lines positioned behind the baseline and across the net behind the ad court service box, as shown in Figure 7.18. Feed a forehand and backhand groundstroke to the first baseline player, who hits each shot to the net player. The first player in the net-play line volleys

each shot to a cross-court target. The groundstroker picks up two balls and moves to the end of the net-play line, the net player moves to end of groundstroke line. After five rounds, move the net-play line to the deuce court so players can work on the opposite strokes.

Sportsmanship Tip
Call Against Yourself (2 minutes)

Explain that players are required to make calls against themselves on double bounces, upon touching the net, or on out balls that an opponent cannot or does not call against the player.

***Volley Workup** (12 minutes).* The object of this game is for players to work up to the feeder's side of the court and stay there as long as possible. Position two players on one baseline to defend the singles court, with the remaining players lined up single-file behind the opposite baseline. One of the baseline pair starts the point with a drop-hit down the center of the court. The first player on the far side, now standing on the service line, moves in to hit a volley and play out the point one against two. If the volleyer wins the point, he or she sprints around the net (to the right), and takes the spot of the nearest baseliner, who moves to her or his right. The baseliner who had been playing the right side runs to the back of the volleying line. If the volleyer loses the point, he or she goes to the end of the volleying line.

Conditioning—Line Sprints *(5 minutes).* See page 59.

Practice Evaluation and Cool-Down *(5 minutes).* Review and evaluate the practice while players perform light stretches. Ask each player to hit 10 volleys in a row against a wall from the forehand and backhand sides before the next practice.

Practice #9

Net Play: The Overhead Smash

Performance Objectives. Players will be able to hit an overhead smash.

Review the Volley. Briefly review the use of the cross-over step and no backswing on the volley.

Introduce the Overhead Smash

"Today we're going to continue to work on our volleys and learn to hit the overhead smash." Briefly explain that an overhead smash is used from the net to "put away" a lob.

Demonstrate the Overhead Smash

Have a player or assistant feed a few easy lobs for you to demonstrate the overhead from a position close to the net.

Explain the Overhead Smash

Describe the elements of the continental (serve) grip, ready position, pivot sideways to the net, racket back past the nose, track the lob with the free hand, adjust position beneath the ball, swing up toward the ball, and follow-through across the body (see Figure 7.19). Point out that the overhead is similar to the serve except that your opponent has placed the ball in the air and you take the racket straight back behind the head instead of using a full swing.

Attend to Players Practicing

Warm-Up Activity: Alternate In With Serve *(4 minutes).* See page 55.

Stretching *(6 minutes).* See pages 30-32.

Figure 7.19 Overhead smash.

Overhead Drills

Overhead Progression *(10 minutes).*   Place 6 to 8 players on a court. On each side of the court (divided by the center service line extended), a retriever stands on one baseline, a feeder at ¾ court, a hitter in the service box across the net, and a shadower on the opposite baseline, as shown in Figure 7.20. The feeder drop-hits three lobs to the hitter, the shadower mimics the hitter, and the retriever picks up the balls. After three hits, the retriever moves to the shadower position, the feeder to the retriever position, the hitter to the feeder position, and the shadower to the hitter position. Have players perform the following progression:

1. Pivot and catch the lob with the free, tracking arm.
2. Hit the overhead into the nearest doubles alley, touch the net, and prepare for the next overhead.
3. Hit one overhead in the air, one off the bounce, and another in the air.

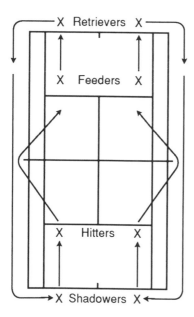

Figure 7.20   Overhead Progression drill.

Volley, Touch, Overhead *(5 minutes).*   Position one player at the net and have the remaining players form a single-file line behind the baseline. Feed two balls to the net player, who hits a volley, touches the net with the racket, hits an overhead, then returns to the end of the line.

Have everyone pick up the balls when the bucket is empty. Each player should perform the drill five times.

Coaching Tip

Most players miss overheads by letting the ball drop too low or by swinging down on the ball. Instruct players to reach up as high as possible for contact and to hit up and out when performing the smash.

Team Lob & Smash Game *(10 minutes).*   Divide the group into teams of lobbers and smashers, who stand well behind the baseline on opposite sides of the net. Two smashers stand at the net and two lobbers on the opposite baseline. A smasher begins the point with an easy drop-hit to either lobber, who must attempt a lob. If a successful return is made using a lob a point is scored for the lobbers. The smashers score a point if the lob is missed or by smashing away a short lob. When the point is completed, two new players from each team move into position to play the next point. The game is completed when one team reaches 11 points; then have teams switch roles.

Team Singles *(10 minutes).*   See page 48.

Sportsmanship Tip
Long Serves (2 minutes)

Tell players that courtesy dictates that they avoid the return of long serves whenever possible by letting the ball pass by them or bumping the ball into the net. Then there will be no confusion over whether the serve was good and players won't risk hitting an opponent who has looked away after seeing the serve was out.

Conditioning—Alley Hops *(5 minutes).*   Players hop over the doubles alley, with both feet together, from singles sideline to doubles sideline and back. Players hop for 20 seconds, then rest for 20 seconds. Take players through this rotation four times.

Practice Evaluation and Cool-Down *(5 minutes).* Review and evaluate the practice while players perform light stretches. Ask each player to hit a minimum of 20 overhead smashes before the next practice.

Error Detection and Correction for the Overhead Smash

ERROR	CORRECTION
1. Backing up to reach a lob	1. Turn sideways by stepping back with the racket-side foot and pivoting on the front foot, then shuffle back
2. Using a full swing	2. Take the racket back "past your nose, not your toes"

Practice #10

Net Play: Coverage

Performance Objective. Players will develop greater consistency and coverage when playing the net.

Review of the Overhead Smash. Briefly review the similarities and differences between the overhead smash and the serve.

Introduce Net Coverage

"After our warm-up and stretch, we're going to continue to work on covering the net."

Demonstrate Net Coverage

From a position halfway between the service line and the net, demonstrate how to use a cross-over step toward the net to hit a forehand or backhand volley and then recover to the ready position.

Explain Net Coverage

Explain that by moving at a 45-degree angle toward the net a player can cut off an opponent's passing shot.

Attend to Players Practicing

Warm-Up Activity: Around-the-World Bump Volleys (4 minutes). Have players form a single-file line at the service line on each side of the net. Instruct the first player in line to "bump" a volley to the first player in the opposite line and quickly go to the end of his or her own line. Challenge players to hit a record number of volleys without letting the ball bounce.

Stretching (6 minutes). See pages 30-32.

Net Coverage Drills

Triangle (5 minutes). Players form a single-file line behind the baseline. The first player in line moves up to the service line, as shown in Figure 7.21. Feed the player a volley near the right sideline, a volley down the center of the court,

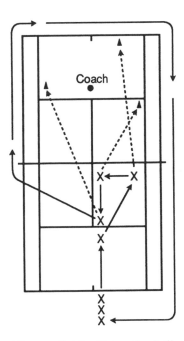

Figure 7.21 Triangle drill.

Practice #10

and an overhead. The player then picks up the three balls and returns to the end of the line. Each player should do the drill five times going to their right. Next, feed the first volley to the players' left so they can work on the opposite strokes.

Alternate In: Groundstroke to Volley (10 minutes). Two players stand at the net with alternates behind the service line and two players at ¾ court across the net with alternates behind the baseline. Players rally cross-court, groundstroke to volley. When a player makes an error, he or she is replaced by an alternate. After several rotations, have the groundstrokers move to the baseline. After 5 minutes, reverse the players' roles so they can work on the opposite shot.

Net Play Workup (10 minutes). See Volley Workup on page 62. Encourage baseline players to mix in lobs and groundstrokes.

Alternate In: Continuous Volley (10 minutes). A player stands in each service box with alternates behind the service lines. Players hit volley to volley (not letting the ball bounce) cross-court. When a player makes an error, she or he is replaced by an alternate.

Sportsmanship Tip
Postmatch Conduct (2 minutes)
Review the proper conduct for both the winner and loser of a match, including shaking hands.

Conditioning—Alley Hops (5 minutes). See page 64.

Practice Evaluation and Cool-Down (5 minutes). Review and evaluate the practice while players perform light stretches. Ask each player to hit 20 consecutive groundstroke-to-volley rallies with a partner from the forehand and backhand sides before the next practice.

Error Detection and Correction for the Net Coverage

ERROR	CORRECTION
Moving parallel to the net to reach a volley	Cross-over step at an angle toward the net to cut off the volley

---

Practice #11

Doubles Play: The Serve & Volley

Performance Objective. Players will begin to charge the net following their first serve in doubles.

Review Net Coverage. Remind players to move at an angle toward the net to cut off passing shots.

Introduce the Serve & Volley

"After the warm-up, we are going to learn the serve & volley tactic for doubles." Point out that the most successful doubles teams are those who rush the net and volley away their opponents' returns.

Demonstrate the Serve & Volley

Demonstrate the serve & volley using a split-step at the service line and volleying cross-court.

Explain the Serve & Volley

Point out that when both players of a doubles team are at the net, they have many more court angles to hit into, which gives them a greater chance of winning the point. Doubles teams that can charge the net behind their serves gain an immediate advantage.

Relate the split-step to a landing in hopscotch. It allows a player to remain balanced while adjusting to volley an oncoming return of serve.

Attend to Players Practicing

Warm-Up Activity: Alternate In, Groundstroke to Volley (4 minutes). See page 66.

Stretching (6 minutes). See pages 30-32.

Serve & Volley (10 minutes). Stand in the deuce court receiving position with one player serving to you, one partnering the server at net, and one as your partner on the ad court service line, as shown in Figure 7.22. The remaining players wait behind the server. The server serves to you and rushes to the net, split-stepping at the service line. Let the serve go by and feed a drop-hit cross-court return. The server volleys the return and the point is played out. Upon completion of the point, the server moves to the net position, the net player runs around to become your partner, and your former partner goes to the end of the serving line.

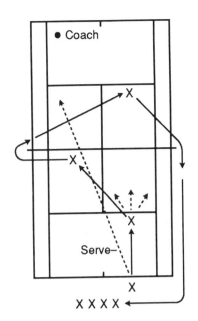

Figure 7.22 Serve and Volley drill.

Safety Tip

Teach doubles partners to shout "Mine" on any balls hit down the middle. The first player to call plays the shot. This prevents both players from swinging at the same ball and possibly injuring each other.

Team Volley Game (10 minutes). Divide the group into two teams, which stand well behind the service line on opposite sides of the net. Two volleyers from each team stand in each service box with teammates behind. Put the ball into play with a drop-hit from outside the doubles alley near the service line. Players play out the point volley to volley, two against two. When the point is completed, two new players from each team move up to the service boxes to play the next point. Team scores are kept, with players rotating after every point.

Monarchs of the Court (15 minutes). This is a progressive workup game in which players play 12-point tie-breaker doubles "matches." The goal of the game is to work to the "top of the hill" and to stay there by beating challengers. Place two doubles teams on each court, and designate one court as the champion's court. All winners will move toward this court (see Figure 7.23). Losers on all but the champion's court remain and serve the next point. Losers on the champion's court go to the end of the line at the beginning of the rotation. Teams waiting to challenge should wait by the net post so they can simply step onto the open side of the court while the champion team gets balls ready to serve.

Error Detection and Correction for Doubles

ERROR	CORRECTION
1. Mistiming the split-step	1. Hopscotch when opponent makes contact with the return
2. Returners try to pass the net players	2. Hit lobs over net rushers' heads and take over the net

Practice #11

Practice #11

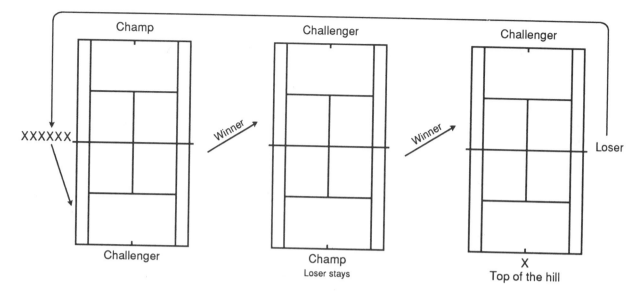

Figure 7.23 Monarchs of the Court drill.

**Sportsmanship Tip
(2 minutes)**

Describe to players how doubles partners can either hinder each other with berating comments or help each other with positive ones ("Don't worry, we'll get the next one." "Hang in there. All we can do is try as hard as we can!").

Conditioning—Toss, Roll, and Catch (5 minutes). See page 55.

Practice Evaluation and Cool-Down (5 minutes). Review and evaluate the practice while players perform light stretches. Ask each player to play one set of doubles before the next practice.

Practice #12

Specialty Shots: Spins

Performance Objectives. Players will begin to develop underspin and topspin groundstrokes and slice serves.

Review of the Serve & Volley. Remind players of the advantage achieved when they follow their serves to the net in doubles.

Introduce the Skill

"Today we will learn three types of spin and how to apply them." Emphasize that one of the marks of a player moving to more advanced tennis is understanding the use of spin.

Demonstrate the Skill

Show players how to hit "ups" with *underspin* by brushing beneath the ball; occasionally let the

ball bounce to show what effect the spin has. Next, demonstrate *topspin* by rolling a ball on the court, then hitting a drop-hit topspin forehand. Finally, hit a *slice* serve to show players how the ball curves through the air.

Explain the Skill

Explain that a ball can be hit with underspin by using a U-shaped (high to low to high) swinging pattern and brushing beneath the ball. Topspin is created by brushing up behind the ball with a low to high swing.

To describe a slice serve, ask players to imagine that there is a face painted on the ball (or actually draw one). Explain that a flat serve is one where the racket hits the "face" on the nose. A slice serve is performed by brushing across the "ear" of the ball. Point out that the continental (serve) grip must be used to accomplish this.

Attend to Players Practicing

Warm-Up Activity: Groundstroke Rallies *(4 minutes)*. See pages 50 and 53.

Stretching *(6 minutes)*.   See pages 30-32.

Ups With Underspin *(2 minutes)*.   Players spread out over the entire court area and perform ups with underspin. Ask them to occasionally let the ball bounce to see the effect of the spin.

Alternate In With Underspin *(5 minutes)*.   Players hit cross-court underspin groundstrokes from the service line.

Topspin Forehand Progression *(10 minutes)*.   Circulate and encourage players to think of brushing up behind the ball as they complete the following progression:

1. Players pin a ball to the top of the net with the racket and then shoot it over the net by pulling the racket straight up to the shoulder (a *net brush*).
2. After five net brushes, players perform five topspin forehands with a drop-hit over the net to a partner.
3. Players perform the Forehand Practice drill (page 49) using topspin forehands.

Slice Serve Practice *(5 minutes)*.   Each player places balls 4 feet from the net, on the service line, at ¾ court, and on the baseline. Instruct players to serve each ball over the net with spin by brushing along the "ear" of the ball, progressing from near the net to the baseline. Once all balls have been hit, players retrieve them and repeat the progression.

Coaching Tip

By this stage of the game many players will have developed strokes with a variety of spins, even without knowing it. Try to build upon these tendencies. Other players will have developed enough pace on serves to be having difficulty controlling them. These players need to add spin to both first and second serves.

Practice

#12

Doubles With Spin *(10 minutes)*.   Divide the group into doubles teams and play regular games, with players required to hit all first serves with spin.

Around-the-World With Topspin *(5 minutes)*.   Divide the team into two equal lines, which stand well behind opposite baselines. The first player in each line stands on the baseline. Feed the ball to one of the baseline players with a drop-hit from outside the doubles alley near the service line. The baseline player must attempt to hit a topspin forehand over the net and run to his or her right to the end of the opposite line. A player making an error receives one "strike." A player with three strikes is eliminated from the game. Play continues until only one player is left.

Conditioning—Line Sprints *(5 minutes)*. (See page 59.)

Practice Evaluation and Cool-Down *(5 minutes)*. Review and evaluate the practice while players perform light stretches. Ask each player to practice slice serving for 20 minutes, mixing in regular serves, before the next practice.

Error Detection and Correction for Spins

ERROR	CORRECTION
1. Hitting spin serves into the net	1. Aim much higher than on a flat serve
2. Spin serve veers too far left or right	2. Adjust targets to account for the spin
3. Rolling the racket over the ball on topspin forehands	3. Brush up behind the ball for topspin
4. Chopping down on the ball on underspin backhands	4a. Keep a firm elbow b. Swing from the shoulder in a U-shaped fashion.

UNIT 8

How Do I Get My Players to Play as a Team?

TEAMWORK

NAME: THE ACES
DRESS: UNIFORM
RULES: +ATTITUDE/BEHAVIOR

SCHEDULE: PRACTICE
GAMES
1. SE...
2. SE...
3. ...

It is very important to emphasize development of individual skills when coaching young tennis players. You can enhance that development by having your youngsters practice and compete as a team.

Building A Tennis Team

The team setting provides an excellent opportunity for youngsters to develop as people and players in a less threatening group situation. USTA National Coaches recommend the following approaches for building a strong, positive team tennis environment.

Choose a Team Name and Motto

Have your players select a name for the team and a motto (e.g., "Face the Pace!") that can be repeated during practices and matches. This will help players feel a special identity with the squad.

Provide a Team Uniform

It's important for players to have some visual identification that shows they belong. Having the same T-shirts or other uniform apparel will make everyone feel a part of the team.

Require Player Support

As a rule, every player should be required to watch teammates' matches in a supportive, positive manner, regardless of the position of the player or importance of the match to the team's overall score. This fosters team loyalty and spirit.

Establish a Team Ritual

Team practices and matches should begin and end with the team in a group and follow a set ritual. You may wish to give a few encouraging words, have the team put their hands together, and repeat the team motto together.

Have Fun Off the Court

Have your team participate in nontennis activities together. Attend a carnival, go to a museum or zoo, take a bike trip, or play another team sport together. This will allow players to get to know each other even better by interacting away from the tennis court.

Prematch Planning

In unit 4 we discussed the importance of planning your practices. Similar preparation is required for team matches. Your team and their opponent will get the most out of the *Junior Team Tennis* match experience if the competition is well organized and well run.

Scheduling

Write down the schedule of play for the upcoming match. It's generally best to schedule doubles matches before singles matches so more kids get to participate on the courts at the start. When you're certain of the match schedule, confirm court availability with the staff of the facility where you will be playing.

Calling the Opposing Coach

Contact the opposing coach at least 2 days before your teams are to play to confirm the date and time of the match, directions to the tennis facility, number of courts to be used, and the schedule of play. In case of threatening weather, stay in touch with the opposing coach to decide on postponement or rescheduling.

Arranging for Transportation

See that all your players get to the matches. Whenever possible, have your team travel to the match together and return together. Organize car pools for away matches, setting departure and arrival times so drivers and players know when and where to meet. Arrange for players to arrive at least 30 minutes before match time so they will have time for a proper warm-up. Players should also be taken home by the same driver.

Making Lineup Decisions

Depending on the format used in your area league, you will probably need to make some decisions as to who will play in what position. You'll need to decide who will play singles, who will play doubles and with whom, and in what order they will compete. Intrasquad scrimmages will help you determine players' relative order of ability, which in turn will help you set your lineup. Remember, one component of the *Junior Team Tennis* philosophy is *Equal Play*, so make sure everyone plays either singles or doubles in each team match.

Match Day Duties

If yours is the home team, arrive at the match site at least 40 minutes before match time.

Checking Facilities and Equipment

Check the courts and nets for cleanliness and repair, get out the tennis balls for play, and make certain that water and a first-aid kit are available.

Communicating With Participants

Greet the opposing team and coach as they arrive and allow them to warm up by sharing courts with your players. Before the start of the match, gather your team for a brief meeting to discuss the lineup, court assignments, and good sportsmanship. Next, gather both teams for the official lineup exchange.

Reporting the Scores

Probably the single greatest headache for a league commissioner is collecting match scores in a timely fashion. To help your commissioner keep accurate and up-to-date records of match results, report all scores *immediately following* the completion of a team match.

Glossary
of Tennis Terms

ace—A ball that is served so well that the opponent cannot return it.

ad (short for *advantage*)—The point scored after deuce. If the serving side scores, it is *ad in*; if the receiving side scores, it is *ad out*.

all—An even score (30-all, 3-all, etc.).

alley—The area between the singles and doubles sidelines on each side of the court. (The singles court is made wider for doubles by the addition of the alley.)

approach—A shot hit just before a player comes to the net that puts the opponent on the defensive.

backcourt—The area between the service line and the baseline.

backhand—The stroke used to return balls hit to the left side of a right-handed player and to the right side of a left-handed player.

choke up—To grip the racket up toward the head.

cross-court shot—A ball hit diagonally across the court.

deep serve—A serve that bounces in the service court near the service line.

deep shot—A shot that bounces in play near the baseline.

deuce—A score of 40-40 (the score is tied and each side has won at least 3 points).

deuce court—The right court, so called because on a deuce score the ball is served there.

double fault—The failure of both service attempts; the server loses the point.

doubles—A match with four players, two on each team.

down-the-line shot—A ball that follows the path of a sideline and is close to it.

drop shot—A ball falling quickly into the forecourt after crossing the net.

fault—A service out.

15—The first point won by a player.

flat shot (flat serve)—A shot that travels in a straight line with little arc and little spin.

foot fault—A fault called against the server for stepping on the baseline or into the court with either foot during the serve.

forecourt—The area between the service line and the net.

forehand—The stroke used to return balls

hit to the right of a right-handed player and to the left of a left-handed player.

40—The score when a player has won 3 points.

game—The part of a set that is completed when one player or side wins 4 points, or 2 points in a row after deuce.

good ball—A ball in play that lands in the court (or on any part of a line forming the boundary of the court).

groundstroke—A stroke, forehand or backhand, made after the ball has bounced.

half-volley—A stroke made by hitting a ball immediately after it has touched on the ground.

let—A point played over because of interference. Also, a serve that hits the top of the net but is otherwise good, in which case the serve is taken again.

lob—A groundstroke that lifts the ball high in the air, usually over the head of the net player.

lob volley—A volleying stroke hit over the head of the opponent.

out—A ball landing outside the boundary lines of the court or, on the serve, outside the boundary lines of the receiver's service court.

Love—Zero (no score).

net game—Play in the forecourt close to the net.

no-ad—A system of scoring a game in which the first player to win 4 points wins the game. If the score reaches 3-all, the next point decides the game.

overhead—A stroke made with the racket above the head.

poach—To hit a ball in doubles, usually at the net, that normally would have been played by one's partner.

point—The smallest unit of score, awarded to a player when the opponent does not make a good return.

rally—A series of good hits made successively by players. Also, the practice procedure in which players hit back and forth to each other.

receiver—The player who receives the service.

serve (short for *service*)—The act of putting the ball into play for each point.

server—The player who serves.

service break—A game won by the opponent of the server.

set—A scoring unit awarded to a player or team who has won (a) six or more games and has a two-game lead, or (b) six games and the tie-break game when played at 6-all.

shot—The hitting of the ball across the net and into the court on the other side.

singles—A match between two players.

smash—A hard overhead shot.

spin—Rotation of the ball.

stroke—The act of striking the ball with the racket.

tie-break game (tie-breaker)—A system used to decide a set when the score is 6-all.

30—The score when a player has won 2 points.

topspin—Forward rotation of the ball caused by brushing from low to high behind the ball.

underspin—The backward rotation of the ball caused by hitting high to low under the ball. Also, backspin or cut.

volley—A stroke made by hitting a ball before it has touched the ground.

Tennis and Coaching Books

Successful Coaching
(USTA Edition)

Rainer Martens, PhD

This special edition of *Successful Coaching*, printed specifically for the USTA and its coaches and instructors, is a comprehensive introduction to the art and science of coaching. Founded on the philosophy "Athletes First, Winning Second," *Successful Coaching* features chapters on communication, motivation, teaching sport skills, conditioning, drug use in sports, and sport management. *Successful Coaching* is the text for the ACEP Leader sport science course.

1990 • Paper • 248 pp • Item PMAR0376 • ISBN 0-88011-376-6 • $16.00

Teaching Tennis: Steps to Success

Jim Brown, PhD

Teaching Tennis: Steps to Success is a comprehensive guide for individualizing and improving tennis instruction. Included are management and safety guidelines, suggestions for identifying and correcting common errors, rating charts for identifying students' skill levels, drill modifications to fit various levels teaching cues to maximize learning, and more. (Note: Tennis instructors will need both *Steps to Success* books to provide students with comprehensive instruction.)

1989 • Paper • 224 pp • Item PBRO0319 • ISBN 0-8011-319-7 • $18.00

Tennis: Steps to Success

Jim Brown, PhD

Tennis: Steps to Success is a breakthrough in sport skill instruction through its development of complete learning progressions—the steps to success. Nineteen steps (chapters) explain concepts and skills, identify the keys to correct technique, give you a summary checklist for evaluating proper technique, and more.

1989 • Paper • 208 pp • Item PBRO0318 • ISBN 0-88011-318-9 • $12.00

The Tennis Drill Book

Sharon Petro, MSA

The author presents over 100 drills for players of all skill levels. Included are tips on groundstroke drills, crosscourt rally, suicide, midcourt drills, short crosscourt, volley drills, lob and overhead drills, and more

1986 • Paper • 128 pp • Item PPET0224 • ISBN 0-88011-224-7 • $10.95

Boris Becker's Tennis
The Making of a Champion

Boris Breskvar in collaboration with Ulrich Kaiser

1987 • Cloth • 128 pp
Item PBRE0290
ISBN 0-88011-290-5 • $15.95

Science of Coaching Tennis

Jack L. Groppel, PhD, James E. Loehr, PhD, D. Scott Melville, PhD, and Ann M. Quinn, MS

1989 • Cloth • 356 pp
Item PGRO0337
ISBN 0-88011-337-5 • $21.00

The Mental ADvantage
Developing Psychological Skills in Tennis

Robert S. Weinberg, PhD

1988 • Paper • 224 pp
Item PWE10293
ISBN 0-88011-293-X • $12.95

Tennis for Advanced Players
And Those Who Would Like To Be

Jack L. Groppel, PhD

1984 • Paper • 208 pp
Item BGRO0072
ISBN 0-87322-072-2 • $12.95

The ACEP Volunteer Level

The ACEP Volunteer Level is for youth sport coaches with limited or no coaching experience. It offers two courses, the Rookie Coaches Course and the Coaching Young Athletes Course. The Rookie Course includes a 3-hour clinic introducing the principles of coaching. Optional sport-specific clinics may also be offered. The Coaching Young Athletes Course includes a 6-hour clinic and provides more comprehensive information concerning developing a positive coaching philosophy, using sport psychology, teaching sport skills, applying sport physiology, and providing sport first aid. For more information on the ACEP Volunteer Level, call the National Center at 1-800-747-4457.